What people are saying

"Here at Citibank we use the Quick Course® computer training book series for 'just-in-time' job aids—the books are great for users who are too busy for tutorials and training. Quick Course® books provide very clear instruction and easy reference."

Bill Moreno, Development Manager
Citibank
San Francisco, CA

"At Geometric Results, much of our work is PC related and we need training tools that can quickly and effectively improve the PC skills of our people. Early this year we began using your materials in our internal PC training curriculum and the results have been outstanding. Both participants and instructors like the books and the measured learning outcomes have been very favorable."

Roger Hill, Instructional Systems Designer
Geometric Results Incorporated
Southfield, MI

"The concise and well-organized text features numbered instructions, screen shots, useful quick reference pointers, and tips…[This] affordable text is very helpful for educators who wish to build proficiency."

Computer Literacy column
Curriculum Administrator Magazine
Stamford, CT

"I have purchased five other books on this subject that I've probably paid more than $60 for, and your [Quick Course®] book taught me more than those five books combined!"

Emory Majors
Searcy, AR

"I would like you to know how much I enjoy the Quick Course® books I have received from you. The directions are clear and easy to follow with attention paid to every detail of the particular lesson."

Betty Weinkauf, Retired Senior
Mission, TX

QUICK COURSE®

in

MICROSOFT®

ACCESS 2000

ONLINE PRESS INC.

Microsoft Press

PUBLISHED BY
Microsoft Press
A Division of Microsoft Corporation
One Microsoft Way
Redmond, WA 98052-6399

Library of Congress Cataloging-in-Publication Data
Quick Course in Microsoft Access 2000 / Online Press Inc.
          p. cm.
       Includes index.
       ISBN 0-7356-1082-7
       ISBN 1-57231-979-8
       1. Microsoft Access. 2. Database management. I. Online Press
   Inc.
       QA76.9.D3Q479 1999
       005.75'65 - - dc21   98-48196
                                                                CIP

Printed and bound in the United States of America.

8 9 10 11 12 QWT 7 6 5 4 3 2

Distributed in Canada by H.B. Fenn and Company Ltd.

A CIP catalogue record for this book is available from the British Library.

Microsoft Press books are available through booksellers and distributors worldwide. For further information about international editions, contact your local Microsoft Corporation office or contact Microsoft Press International directly at fax (425) 936-7329. Visit our Web site at www.microsoft.com/mspress. Send comments to *mspinput@microsoft.com*.

A Quick Course® Education/Training Edition for this title is published by Online Training Solutions, Inc. (OTSI). For information about supplementary workbooks, contact OTSI at 15442 Bel-Red Road, Redmond, WA 98052, USA, 1-800-854-3344. E-mail: quickcourse@ otsiweb.com.

Authors: Joyce Cox, Nathan Dudley, and Liz Aune
Acquisitions Editor: Susanne M. Forderer
Project Editor: Anne Taussig

From the publisher

Quick Course®... The name says it all.

In today's busy world, everyone seems to be looking for easier methods, faster solutions, and shortcuts to success. That's why we decided to publish the Quick Course® series.

Why Choose A Quick Course®?

When all the computer books claim to be fast, easy, and complete, how can you be sure you're getting exactly the one that will do the job for you? You can depend on Quick Course® books because they give you:

- Everything you need to do useful work, in two easy-to-tackle parts: "Learning the Basics" (for beginning users) and "Building Proficiency" (for intermediate users).

- Easy-to-follow numbered instructions and thorough explanations.

- To-the-point directions for creating professional-looking documents that can be recycled and customized with your own data.

- Numerous screen shots to help you follow along when you're not at the computer.

- Handy pointers to key terms and tasks for quick lookup and review.

- Consistent quality—the same team of people creates them all. If you like one, you'll like the others!

We at Microsoft Press are proud of our reputation for producing quality products that meet the needs of our readers. We are confident that this Quick Course® book will live up to your expectations.

Jim Brown,
Publisher

Content overview

PART ONE: LEARNING THE BASICS

We set the stage with an explanation of basic database concepts and then show you how to create a table and enter records. Then you edit the table, change its appearance, and print it. You also see how to get help and quit Access.

You customize a table's structure, including setting field properties to control what data can be entered and how it looks. Then you see how to use forms to enter and review data. Finally, you customize a form in design view.

You learn techniques for extracting information from a database with the Find command, filters, queries, reports, and data access pages. We also show you how to create and customize a switchboard to help others easily find what they need.

PART TWO: BUILDING PROFICIENCY

We give three basic rules for database design and introduce other tools that help you build less error-prone databases. Then you create relationships so that you can work with multiple tables. Finally, we discuss data protection.

You create multi-table forms and then add subforms, command buttons, and field formulas. We then demonstrate ways you can use forms and queries together to increase data-input efficiency and better display extracted data.

After a discussion of updating switchboards, we deal with the maintenance of a database and how to use action queries to manipulate multiple records simultaneously. Then we briefly describe how to secure a database that has multiple users.

Content details

PART TWO: BUILDING PROFICIENCY

PART ONE

LEARNING THE BASICS

In Part One, we teach you the basic techniques for working with Microsoft Access 2000. After completing the first three chapters, you will be prepared to work with most of the databases you'll create with Access. In Chapter 1, you learn some key concepts and then create a simple table. In Chapter 2, you refine the table by customizing its structure, and you use forms to enter and view data. Finally, in Chapter 3, you use queries and reports to find and extract the information you need from your database.

1

Simple Database Tables

We set the stage with an explanation of basic database concepts and then show you how to create a table and enter records. Then you edit the table, change its appearance, and print it. You finish the chapter by learning ways to get help and how to quit Access.

The basic structure of the table created in Chapter 1 can be used to catalog almost any set of information, including student contact information or client details.

Table created and concepts covered:

*Let Access generate
a sequential number
as the primary key*

*Size columns
to see complete
entries*

*Save time by letting Access
enter parentheses and
hyphens for you*

Customers   7/1/99

Customer ID	First Name	Last Name	Address	City	State	Postal Code	Phone Number
1	Art	Kansaw	123 Traveller Trail	Hollywood	CA	11403-	(213) 555-1111
2	Ellen	Noy	1171 Windy Way	Hollywood	CA	11403-	(213) 555-9297
3	Cal	Orado	5941 Skiers Haven	Hollywood	CA	11403-	(213) 555-0909
5	Ida	Hough	5454 Russet Road	Hollywood	CA	11403-	(213) 555-6819

Page 1

*Sort any column
by clicking a button
on the toolbar*

*Print in portrait or
landscape mode,
depending on your data*

Y ou have probably just started to work with Microsoft Access 2000 and are excited but nervous about learning to use this powerful database tool. You are hoping that, like other Windows applications, Access will be simple to use and yet offer you the power you need to handle complex data. Well, relax. By the end of this chapter, you'll know how to create database tables, enter data, and move around within the program. If you have used other database applications, a quick review of this chapter will get you going.

Throughout this book, we focus on how to use Access to carry out common database tasks, and for our examples, we show you how to create a database for a small video store. We assume that you have already installed both Microsoft Windows and Access on your computer. We also assume that you have worked with Windows before and that you know how to start programs, move windows, choose commands from menus, highlight text, and so on. If you are a new Windows user, we suggest you take a look at *Quick Course® in Microsoft Windows*, another book in our series, which will help you quickly come up to speed. And finally, we assume you are using a mouse. You can perform many Access functions using the keyboard, but a mouse is required for some tasks.

It's time to get started, so let's fire up Access:

Starting Access

1. Click the Start button, click Programs, and then choose Microsoft Access from the Programs submenu. After a few seconds, you see a dialog box like the one on the facing page.

Other ways of starting Access

Instead of starting Access from the Start menu, you can create a shortcut icon for Access on the Windows desktop. Right-click an open area of the desktop and choose New and then Shortcut from the shortcut menu. In the Create Shortcut dialog box, simply click the Browse button and navigate to the folder where the msaccess.exe program is stored, probably C:\Program Files\Microsoft Office\Office. Select the program, click Open, and then click Next. Type a name for the shortcut icon and then click Finish. Double-click the icon to start Access. For maximum efficiency, you can start Access and open an existing database by choosing the database from the Documents submenu of the Start menu, where Windows stores the names of up to 15 of the most recently opened files. If you are using Microsoft Office, you can choose Open Office Document from the top of the Start menu and navigate to the folder in which the database you want to open is stored. To start Access and open a new database, choose New Office Document from the top of the Start menu, and then double-click the Blank Database icon.

2. If necessary, click the Office Assistant's Start Using Microsoft Access option. (We discuss the Office Assistant on page 27. As you work through this chapter, the Office Assistant may entertain you with some cute antics and may display a message or a light bulb. Other than responding to messages by clicking an option, you can ignore it for now.)

3. Click the Blank Access Database option and click OK.

4. When Access displays the File New Database dialog box, click Cancel to close the dialog box so that you can examine an empty Microsoft Access window like this one:

Different configurations

We wrote this book using a computer running Microsoft Windows 98 with the screen resolution set to 800x600. If you are using a different version of Windows or a different resolution, you might notice slight differences in the appearance of your screens. We are also using the Access configuration that results when you do a Typical installation of Microsoft Office 2000 from CD-ROM. Don't be alarmed if your setup is different from ours. You will still be able to follow along with most of the examples in this book. You'll notice that we've hidden the Windows taskbar. (Right-click a blank area of the taskbar, choose Properties, click Auto-Hide, and click OK.)

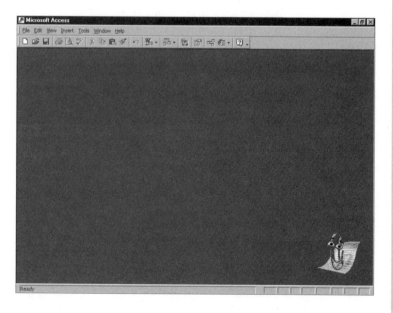

Like most Windows applications, the Access window has a title bar at the top and a status bar at the bottom. You also see the menu bar and toolbar, which you use to give Access instructions. Because these bars work a little differently from those you might have used in other Windows applications, we'll quickly take a look at them now.

The menu bar →

The *menu bar* changes to reflect the menus and commands for the database component you are working with. You use standard Windows techniques to choose a command from a menu or submenu and to work with dialog boxes. However, Access 2000 goes beyond the basic Windows procedure for choosing commands by determining which commands you are most likely to use and adjusting the display of commands on each menu to reflect how you use the program. As a quick example, let's take a look at the View menu:

1. Click *View* on the menu bar to drop down the View menu. The two arrows at the bottom of the menu indicate that one or more commands are hidden because they are not the ones most people use most of the time.

Expanding menus →

2. Continue pointing to the word *View*. The two arrows disappear and more commands appear on the menu. (You can also click the two arrows to make hidden commands appear.) The status of a less frequently used command is indicated by a lighter shade of gray. If you choose one of the light gray commands, in the future it will no longer be hidden and will appear in the same color as the other commands.

3. Move the pointer away from the menu bar and the menu before pressing Esc twice to deactivate them both.

Shortcut menus

Shortcut menus group together the commands used most frequently with a specific type of object, such as a database field or a window element. You display a shortcut menu by pointing to the object and clicking the right mouse button. You can then choose a command from the menu in the usual way.

The other way to give Access an instruction is to click a button on a *toolbar*. This is the equivalent of choosing the corresponding command from a menu and if necessary, clicking OK to accept all the default settings in the command's dialog box. Access comes with several built-in toolbars, equipped with buttons that help you accomplish specific tasks, and Access automatically displays whichever toolbar you need to work with the active database component. Currently, you see the Database toolbar with all but three buttons dimmed to indicate that they are unavailable.

By default, the toolbar sits under the menu bar above the workspace, but if it gets in your way, you can move it anywhere on the screen. Let's do some exploring:

1. Point to each button on the toolbar. Access's *ScreenTips* feature displays a box with the button's name.

ScreenTips

2. Point to the toolbar's move handle—the light gray bar at the left end of the toolbar. When the pointer changes to a four-headed arrow, drag the toolbar over the workspace, where it becomes a floating toolbar, like this one:

Moving the toolbar

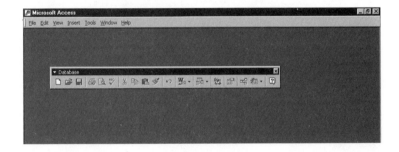

3. Now point to the floating toolbar's title bar and drag to the right side of the screen. The toolbar "docks" itself along the edge of the window, the title bar disappears, and the move handle reappears at the top of the bar.

4. Point to the move handle and drag the toolbar back up under the menu bar.

Now that you know how to give Access instructions, let's discuss the concept of a database.

What Is a Database?

A database is a structured collection of data items. Because the data's arrangement is predictable, you can manipulate the items to extract useful information. The most basic component of an Access database is a *table* in which information is arranged in *rows* and *columns*. In addition to tables, an Access database can include queries, forms, reports, data access pages

Personalized menus

Access's menus adjust themselves to the way you work, making more commands available as you use them. The commands that you don't use are hidden so they don't get in the way. As a result, your menus may not look exactly like ours, and occasionally, we may tell you to choose a command that is not visible. When this happens, don't panic. Simply pull down the menu and wait for all its commands to be displayed.

(for Web viewing), and other components, all of which allow you to view and manipulate the information in your database in a variety of ways. As you progress through this book, we will introduce each of these components.

In this chapter, you'll create a table to hold information about a video store's customers. But first, let's take a look at a sample database for a company called Northwind Traders, which comes with Access. (You can follow along with these steps only if you have installed the sample databases. If you have not, simply read this example.)

The Open button

1. Click the Open button on the toolbar to see this dialog box:

Managing files

To print, delete, rename, or move a database from Access's Open dialog box, simply right-click its filename in the Open dialog box and choose a command from the shortcut menu. You can perform most of these tasks from the File New Database dialog box as well. You can also click the Tools button on the dialog box's toolbar to drop down a menu that contains the Delete and Rename commands.

Finding files

Suppose you can't remember what you called a database or where you stored it. In the Open dialog box, click the Tools button, click Find, enter the appropriate drive in the Look In box, click the Search Subfolders check box, and check that File Name is selected in the Property edit box. Select the appropriate option in the Condition edit box and then enter any part of the filename you remember in the Value edit box. Click Add To List to add your criteria to the criteria list and then click Find Now. Access searches this drive and its subfolders for any Access database with the Value entry in its filename and lists the ones it finds. You can then select the database you want and click Open. If you have many databases with similar names, refine the search by specifying other properties such as text in the database or its date of modification. To save searches, click the Save Search button, name the search, and click OK.

2. Move to the Program Files\Microsoft Office\Office\Samples folder. If it is available, double-click Nwind.mdb; otherwise, click Cancel. (If a message box informs you that the database is read-only, click OK.) If a window introducing Northwind Traders appears, click OK. You then see this window:

The *objects bar* on the left contains icons representing the components of the Northwind database. The Tables icon is active, and the database's tables are listed on the right.

The objects bar

The Database window's
Open button

3. Select Employees in the list of tables and click the Open button on the Database window's toolbar. Your screen looks like this:

Row header   *Column header*

Table menu bar
Table Datasheet toolbar

New Record

Record navigator

Fields and records

Access displays a different toolbar and opens the table in a new Table window. The table consists of items of information arranged in columns, called *fields*, which have headings, called *field names*, which describe the type of information in each column. Each item of information is a *field value*, and each row of items is a *record*. In this table, each record consists of all the field values for a specific employee.

4. Scroll sideways using the scroll bar at the bottom of the Table window. Notice the fields contain numbers, text, and dates.

Let's close the Northwind database and start a new one:

Closing tables

1. Click the Table window's Close button to close the window.

2. Now click the Database window's Close button.

Setting Up a Database

As you work through this book, you'll create a database for a video store owned by Mr. and Mrs. Mitch Egan. Before you can enter any information, you need to set up the database so that Access can store all the tables, queries, forms, reports, and data access pages you'll create in one file. Follow these steps:

The New button

1. Click the New button to display this dialog box:

Ready-made databases

Access includes several sample databases that can give you ideas on how to construct your own databases or that you can customize. To use a sample database, click the Access Database Wizards, Pages, And Projects option in the Microsoft Access dialog box (see page 5), and click OK, or click the New button. Then on the Databases tab of the New dialog box, double-click any database to have Access walk you through its construction.

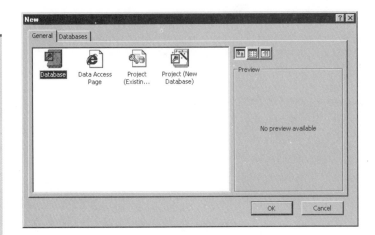

2. With Database selected on the General tab, click OK to open the File New Database dialog box, and then click the My Documents icon on the shortcuts bar. The dialog box now looks something like this:

The My Documents icon

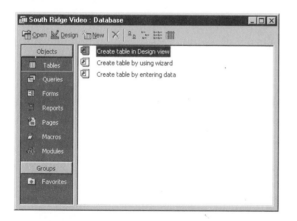

3. If necessary, select db1 in the File Name edit box by double-clicking it, type *South Ridge Video*, and click Create. Access opens this Database window for South Ridge Video:

Creating a Table

You want to create your first table, which will be used to maintain customer information. You could open a blank table and then customize it, but there's an easier way to get started. Instead of creating the table from scratch, let's get one of the

Storing elsewhere

To store a file in a folder other than My Documents, click the arrow to the right of the Save In box and use the drop-down list to find the folder you want. Double-click it to open it and then click Create. You can also use the icons on the shortcuts bar to access folders you use often. To make a new folder, click the Create New Folder button. To change the default folder, choose Options from the Tools menu and change the entry in the Default Database Folder edit box on the General tab.

Access wizards to help. A *wizard* is a tool that walks you through the process of creating a standard Access component, such as a table, form, query, report, or data access page. (You don't have to use the wizards, but when you are first learning Access, they are a great way to quickly produce components.) Follow these steps:

The Database window's New button

1. In the Database window, click the New button. Access opens a dialog box where you specify how you want to create the table:

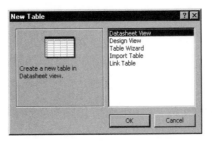

You could double-click one of the options in the Database window to create a new table, but we took this route to show you that you can also import a table created in another application or create a table that is linked to one in another file.

The Table Wizard

2. Click Table Wizard and then click OK to display the first of a series of dialog boxes that lead you through the steps of creating your table's field structure:

Ready-made business and personal tables

In the first Table Wizard dialog box, you can choose from a variety of sample tables used in business and at home. The business tables are listed by default. If you click the Personal option, Access displays a list of sample tables you can create for personal use.

3. In the Sample Tables list, click Customers. The Sample Fields list changes to reflect the kind of information usually stored in a customer table, with CustomerID selected.

4. Click the > button to add the CustomerID field name to the Fields In My New Table list.

5. Select ContactFirstName and click the > button.

6. With ContactFirstName selected in the Fields In My New Table list, click Rename Field to display this dialog box: ← **Renaming predefined fields**

7. Type *First Name* and click OK.

8. Add ContactLastName to the Fields In My New Table list and rename it as *Last Name*.

9. Add the BillingAddress, City, StateOrProvince, PostalCode, and PhoneNumber fields. Then rename BillingAddress as *Address* and StateOrProvince as *State*, and click Next to display the following wizard dialog box:

If you change your mind about a selection you made in an earlier wizard dialog box, click the Back button to retrace your steps, correct your mistake, and click Next to move forward again. You can cancel the whole process by clicking the Cancel button, and you can complete the process with the default entries in all the dialog boxes by clicking the Finish button.

Setting your own primary key

If you set the primary key yourself, none of the entries in the primary-key field can be exactly the same. If you try to enter the same field value in the primary-key field of two records, Access displays an error message and won't let you move to a new record until you change the duplicate in the record you are currently entering.

The primary key ———————►

10. The name Access suggests for this database—Customers—is logical, so don't change the entry in the edit box. Let Access set the *primary key*, which is a field that distinguishes one record from another. When you allow Access to create the primary key, Access designates the first field of the table as the primary key and makes it an AutoNumber field. Then a consecutive number will be entered as that field's value for each new record. Click Next to display this wizard dialog box:

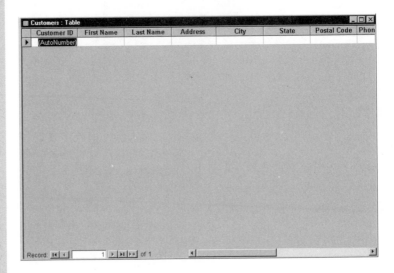

11. You want to enter data directly in the table, so click the Finish button without changing the selected option. Access goes to work setting up the table with the field names you have specified and then displays this Table window:

The table's structure

When you use the Table Wizard to create a new table, it sets up the table's structure by assigning names to the fields, determining their data type, allocating sizes, and setting various other properties that control the data you enter in the table. This behind-the-scenes structure is most visible in the Phone Number field, where the wizard has specified that you can enter a maximum of ten digits. These digits will appear in the table with the first three digits enclosed in parentheses and the sixth and seventh digits separated by a hyphen. We discuss the underlying structure of tables and how to manipulate it on page 32.

Entering Records in a Table

Each record in the Customers table will contain information about one customer. In Access, you can enter and edit records either directly in the table or in a form. We'll look at tables in this section and cover forms in Chapter 2.

To enter records in a table, you must first display the table in *datasheet view*. Because you told the Table Wizard that you wanted to enter data directly in the table, Access automatically switched the new table to datasheet view. The arrowhead in the *record selector* (the gray box at the left end of the first row) indicates that the first record is ready to receive data. In the first field of this record, Access has inserted (AutoNumber) to indicate that the program will automatically insert a sequential number in this primary-key field to distinguish this record from all others in the table.

Datasheet view

The record selector

Follow these steps to enter three records in the database:

1. Press Enter to confirm (AutoNumber) as the first field's value and move to the next field. Then type *Art* as the First Name field value. The arrowhead in the row selector changes to a pencil, indicating that the data in the record has been changed but not yet saved. (Access has added a second record with an asterisk in its row selector, indicating that the new record is empty.) Press Enter to move to the next field.

2. Enter these field values in the first record, pressing Enter after each value:

First Name	Last Name	Address	City	State	Postal Code	Phone Number
	Kansaw	123 Traveller Trail	Hollywood	CA	11403	2135551111

In the Postal Code field, Access appends a hyphen to the value. In the Phone Number field, the program puts parentheses around the area code and a hyphen after the 5s (the tip on the facing page tells you why). When you press Enter after typing the phone number, Access moves the insertion point to the first field of the next record.

3. Enter two more records, again pressing Enter after each value:

First Name	Last Name	Address	City	State	Postal Code	Phone Number
Ellen	Noy	1171 Windy Way	Hollywood	CA	11403	2135559297
Cal	Orado	5941 Skiers Haven	Hollywood	CA	11403	2135550909

Shouldn't you save your work now? You don't have to, because Access has already taken care of that chore for you. Unlike many applications that wait for you to tell them when to save information, Access saves the values in a new or edited record as soon as you move to another record.

Moving Around a Table

Scrolling

You can move around a table using either the mouse or the keyboard. Like most Windows programs, Access automatically adds scroll bars along the bottom and right sides of the window if the table is too wide or too tall to be displayed in its entirety. You can click the scroll arrows to move to the left or right one field at a time or up or down one record at a time. Click on either side of the scroll box to move one windowful of records at a time.

The record indicator

As well as using the scroll bars, you can click the buttons on either side of the *record indicator* at the bottom of the window to move among records. The Previous Record and Next Record buttons—the left and right arrowheads—move you through the table one record at a time, and the First Record and Last Record buttons—the arrowheads pointing to a solid line—move you to the first and last record in the table. The New Record button—the arrowhead pointing to an asterisk—moves you to the first field of the empty record after the last record.

Moving with the mouse

Moving with the keyboard

You can move the insertion point to a specific field by clicking the desired location. To select an entire field, click its left border (the pointer will be shaped like a fat cross). Once you have selected a field, you can move to adjacent fields by pressing the Arrow keys. In fact, using the keyboard is often the fastest way to move around a table. A list of the keys you can use is shown on the facing page.

Use this key...	To move...
Tab	Horizontally one field at a time
Right and Left Arrows	When a field is highlighted, horizontally one field at a time; otherwise, moves the insertion point one character at a time
Up and Down Arrows	Vertically one field at a time
Home	To the first field in the current record
End	To the last field in the current record
Ctrl+Home	To the first field in the first record
Ctrl+End	To the last field in the last record
Page Down	Down one windowful of records
Page Up	Up one windowful of records
Ctrl+Page Down	To the right one windowful of fields
Ctrl+Page Up	To the left one windowful of fields

Practice moving around the Customers table using the mouse and keyboard. Knowing various navigational methods is useful because you can then select the method most appropriate for a particular situation. As you can imagine, the ability to jump to the beginning or end of a table and to move through records a windowful at a time is especially useful with tables that contain thousands of records.

Changing the Table's Data

If your data were a simple list that didn't change, you could keep it on paper. But data is often dynamic, and you need to be able to delete, insert, and otherwise change records to keep a database current. Here we show you how to edit the values in individual fields and insert and delete entire records.

Editing Fields

If you make a mistake while entering a field value, you can use the Backspace key to delete the error and then retype the value. If you discover a mistake later, you can click an insertion point in the offending field and use normal editing techniques. You can also use one or two editing tricks as you enter values. Follow the steps on the next page.

Jumping to a specific record

If you know the number of the record you want to work with, you can select the number currently displayed in the record indicator box. Then type the new number (not the autonumber in the primary-key field, but the number describing the record's relative position: 1 of 2, 4 of 5, etc.) and press Enter.

The New Record button

1. If necessary, click the New Record button on the toolbar to move to the empty record at the end of the table, and then press Enter to move to the First Name field.

Duplicating values

2. Press Ctrl+' (single quotation mark). Access duplicates the value from the same field of the preceding record in the active field. Press Enter.

Within a table, you can also duplicate values by copying and pasting them. Try this:

The Copy button

1. Select the Last Name value in the third record by clicking its left border, and click the Copy button on the toolbar.

The Paste button

2. Then select the Last Name field in the fourth record by clicking its left border, and click the Paste button.

3. Use either the Ctrl+' or copy-and-paste technique to copy the rest of the field values from the third record into the fourth record.

Now let's edit the fourth record:

1. Double-click Orado in the fourth record, replace the highlighted value by typing *Fornia*, and press Enter to highlight the next field.

Copying and pasting cautions

Copying and pasting one field value is simple enough, but complications can arise when copying multiple fields. After selecting the fields and clicking the Copy button, you must select the same number of fields before clicking the Paste button. Be careful to paste the field values into fields that have the same properties as the source fields; otherwise data may be lost or Access may refuse to complete the operation. If Access encounters problems, it alerts you and puts the offending values in a Paste Errors table, which you can then evaluate for troubleshooting clues.

2. Type *104 American Avenue*, press Enter, type *Beverly Hills*, but don't press Enter. The table now looks like this:

Customer ID	First Name	Last Name	Address	City	State	Postal Code	Phon
1	Art	Kansaw	123 Traveller Tra	Hollywood	CA	11403-	(213)
2	Ellen	Noy	1171 Windy Wa	Hollywood	CA	11403-	(213)
3	Cal	Orado	5941 Skiers Ha	Hollywood	CA	11403-	(213)
4	Cal	Fornia	104 American A	Beverly Hills	CA	11403-	(213)
(AutoNumber)							

Record: 4 of 4

3. Restore the original value in the City field by pressing Ctrl+Z. ←

Undoing edits

4. Here's another way to undo an entry: With Hollywood high-lighted, type *Malibu* in the City field and then press Esc.

5. Press Esc again to restore the original values to all the fields in the record.

Inserting and Deleting Records

To insert a new record in a table, you can click the empty record designated by the asterisk at the end of the table and enter your data. (As you've seen, you can also move quickly to this empty record by clicking the New Record button on the tool-bar.) Here's another way to insert a new record:

1. Choose Data Entry from the Records menu. Access displays a ←
single record in which you enter your data, as shown here:

Inserting a record

2. Press Enter to accept (AutoNumber), and then type the follow-ing data, pressing Enter after each field:

First Name	Last Name	Address	City	State	Postal Code	Phone Number
Ida	Hough	5454 Russet Road	Hollywood	CA	11403	2135556819

3. Choose Remove Filter/Sort from the Records menu to see the entire table. (We talk about filters on page 58 and about sort-ing on page 23.) The new record has been added to the bottom

of the table to maintain sequential order in the primary-key Customer ID field.

Deleting a record

To delete a record, you simply select the record and click the Delete Record button. Follow these steps to delete the duplicate record for Cal Orado from the Customers table:

The Delete Record button

1. Select the fourth record by clicking its record selector, and click the Delete Record button on the toolbar or press the Delete key. The Office Assistant displays this message:

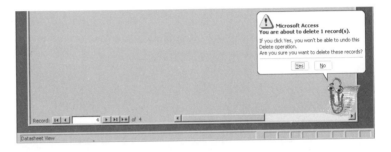

2. Click Yes. Access deletes the record and updates the table.

Caution!

Be careful when deleting records. If you make a mistake and delete the wrong record, you can't restore the record by clicking an Undo button or choosing Undo from the Edit menu after you've confirmed the deletion.

Changing the Table's Appearance

Like most people, you're probably more interested in using database tables to store the information you need than in making your data look fancy, but sometimes a little customization can actually make tables easier to work with. This type of customization changes the way the table looks but doesn't alter its data.

Sizing Windows, Columns, and Rows

To see the information in a table, you may have to enlarge the Table window or adjust the sizes of fields. Perhaps you've noticed that as you move your mouse around the screen, the pointer sometimes changes shape. On the frame of a window, on the gridlines between the field names, and on the dividing lines between the row selectors, the pointer changes to various

Deleting records with an AutoNumber field

When you delete a record in a table that has an AutoNumber field, Access does not update the remaining fields' sequential numbers. Once a number has been assigned to a record, that number is never used again, and deleting a record leaves a gap in the sequential order of the values in the AutoNumber field.

kinds of double-headed arrows. While the pointer has this shape, you can resize the Table window or the fields.

To resize the window, simply point to its frame, and when the pointer changes to a double-headed arrow, hold down the left mouse button and drag the frame to decrease or increase the window's size.

Sizing windows

Resizing fields is equally simple, as you'll see as you follow these steps:

1. Move the pointer to the gridline between the Address and City field names.

Sizing columns

2. When the pointer changes to a double-headed arrow, hold down the left mouse button and drag to the right. When the line attached to the pointer is about where you want the field's border to be, release the mouse button.

3. Point to the dividing line between the first and second row selectors and drag downward to increase the heights of all the fields in all the records. (You can't adjust the height of only one record.)

Sizing rows

Here's another way to change the widths of fields:

1. Scroll the table until the last four fields are visible. Move the pointer to the City field name, and when the pointer changes to a downward-pointing arrow, click to select that field in all records. Then move the pointer to the Phone Number field name, hold down the Shift key, and click to add the State, Postal Code, and Phone Number fields to the selection.

Selecting multiple columns

2. Choose Column Width from the Format menu to display the dialog box shown below:

Column Width		? ✕
Column Width: 15.6667		OK
☑ Standard Width		Cancel
		Best Fit

3. Type *15* and press Enter to change the widths of all four fields at the same time.

Fast column width adjustment

Clicking an insertion point in a field, choosing the Column Width command from the Format menu, and clicking the Best Fit button adjusts the width of the column to fit its widest field value. You can also double-click the gridline to the right of the field name's column header.

The Format menu also includes a Row Height command that allows you to set the heights of the rows precisely. Here's how to restore the original heights of the rows:

Restoring row height

1. Choose Row Height from the Format menu to display this dialog box:

2. Click the Standard Height check box and then click OK.

3. Next click any field to remove the highlighting.

4. You might want to practice resizing the fields of the Customers table. When you have finished experimenting, use any method to decrease the width of the columns so that you can see all of them at the same time.

Moving Fields

By default, the fields are displayed in the order in which you entered them when you created the table. You can change the field order by selecting a field's column and dragging it to a new position. For example, if you want to look up a customer's phone number, it might be useful to see the Phone Number field next to the customer names. Follow these steps to move the Phone Number field:

1. Click the Phone Number field name once to select the entire column.

2. Point to the Phone Number field name, hold down the left mouse button, and drag the field to the left. As you move the field, Access highlights the dividing lines between columns to indicate the new position of the Phone Number field.

3. When the dividing line to the right of the Last Name field is highlighted, release the mouse button. The Phone Number field is shown in its new position on the facing page.

Freezing and hiding fields

While scrolling other fields, you can freeze a single field in position. Click anywhere in the field and choose Freeze Columns from the expanded Format menu. The field moves to the left to become the first column in the table. You can then scroll the remaining fields. Choose Unfreeze All Columns from the Format menu to remove the freeze, and then, if necessary, drag the column back to its original location. To freeze a set of fields, click the first field in the set, hold down the Shift key, click the last field, and then choose Freeze Columns. You can hide fields by selecting them and choosing Hide Columns from the Format menu. To redisplay the fields, choose Unhide Columns from the Format menu, click the check boxes for the fields you want to redisplay, and then click Close to exit the Unhide Columns dialog box.

4. For more practice, move the Phone Number field back to its original position to the right of the Postal Code field.

Sorting Records

The Customers table is short enough that you can view all its records at one time in the window. But database tables can contain several hundred or even several thousand records. When working with a large table, you may want to sort the table on a particular field. Here's how to sort the records of the Customers table based on the Last Name field:

1. Click anywhere in the Last Name column and then click the Sort Ascending button on the toolbar to sort starting with A (or the lowest digit). Click the Sort Descending button to sort starting with Z (or the highest digit).

The Sort Ascending and Sort Descending buttons

2. Restore the original order by clicking anywhere in the Customer ID column and clicking the Sort Ascending button.

To sort the records on more than one column, you must first arrange the columns so that they are side-by-side in the table in the order of the sort. For example, to sort a mailing list in ascending order by state and then by city, you first move the State column to the left of the City column. Then you select both the columns and click the Sort Ascending button. Access sorts the records first by state and then by city within each

Sorting on more than one column

state. After the sort, you can move the State column back to the right of the City column.

Other Customizable Options

You can customize several parts of the Access window, as well as control other table functions and properties, by choosing the Options command from the Tools menu. You won't make any changes now, but let's take a look at the dialog box that Access displays when you choose this command:

1. Choose Options from the Tools menu to display the dialog box shown here:

Changing cell attributes

As well as changing the font used to display values in datasheet view, you can change the look of the "cells" containing the field values. For example, the gridlines that separate the columns and rows in an Access table are optional. You can remove them by choosing the Datasheet command from the Format menu and then deselecting the Horizontal and Vertical check boxes in the Gridlines Shown section of the Datasheet Formatting dialog box. Other options control the look of the cells, as well as their color.

As you can see, the Options dialog box has several tabs, and clicking a tab displays a category of options.

2. For now, take a careful look at what's available for each category so that as you use Access you'll know where to go if you want to change an option. Then click Cancel.

Changing the Font

One way to change the look of a table is to change the font used for the field values. You may have noticed in the Options dialog box that the Datasheet tab has several fonts available for you to choose from. You can also change the font, size, and style of the entire table by using menu commands. Follow these steps:

1. Choose Font from the Format menu to display the Font dialog box shown here:

Your font list may be different from ours depending on your printer and the programs installed on your computer.

2. In the Font Style section, click Bold, and then click OK to see the result. All the field values in the table are now bold. (You cannot use the Font command to change only part of the table.)

Making field values bold

3. Go ahead and experiment with some of the font options to see how easily you can change the font and font size and draw lines under field values to make them stand out. Return the table to its original settings—Arial, Regular, and 10, with no underline—when you've finished.

Printing Tables

Sometimes you might need a printed copy of a database table for use away from your computer. Before you print, however, you will want to check the layout of the table so that you print in the most efficient way. Otherwise, you may find a table spreading across several pages when a little planning could have kept the table to one or two pages. Follow these steps to check the layout of the Customers table:

1. Click the Print Preview button on the toolbar to display page 1 of the database table, as shown on the next page.

The Print Preview button

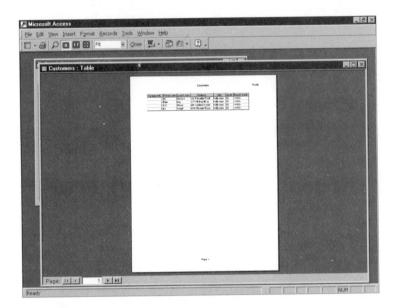

2. Click the Next Page button to the right of the page indicator in the bottom left corner of the window to view the second page, or click the Two Pages button on the Print Preview toolbar to see the first and second pages side by side.

The Two Pages button

To make the entire table fit on one page, you can adjust the page layout in a variety of ways. Try this:

Adjusting page layout

1. Choose Page Setup from the File menu to see this dialog box:

Setting margins

You can adjust the settings on the Margins tab to manipulate the position of the data and how much will print on one page.

2. Click the Page tab to display its options, click Landscape to print the table sideways on the page, and click OK. The print preview window now shows that the table fits on one page.

Changing page orientation

To print one copy of the entire table, all you have to do is click the Print button on the toolbar. If you want to print more than one copy or only part of a table, here's what you do:

The Print button

1. Choose Print from the File menu to display the dialog box shown below, which looks similar to those used by most Windows applications:

```
Print                                              ? X
  Printer
    Name:    HP DeskJet 682C                ▼    Properties
    Status:  Default printer; Ready
    Type:    HP DeskJet 680C Series Printer
    Where:   LPT1:
    Comment:                                      ☐ Print to File

  Print Range                    Copies
    ⦿ All                          Number of Copies:    1 ⬍
    ○ Pages From:     To:
    ○ Selected Record(s)           [1][2][3]  ☐ Collate

    Setup...                         OK        Cancel
```

2. Make your selections and click OK. (If you decide not to print, click Cancel or the Close button.) Your printed results should look like those shown at the beginning of the chapter.

3. Click the Close button on the PrintPreview toolbar to leave print preview.

Getting Help

This has been a whistle-stop tour of Access tables, and you might not remember everything we've covered. If you forget how to carry out a particular task, help is never far away. You can use the ScreenTips feature to jog your memory about the functions of toolbar buttons. And you may have noticed that dialog boxes contain a Help button—the ? at the right end of the title bar—you can click to get information about their options. Here you'll look at ways to get information using the Office Assistant. Follow the steps on the next page.

Using the Web for help

If you have a modem and are connected to the Internet, you can quickly access Microsoft's Web site to get help or technical support. Simply choose Office On The Web from the Help menu to start your Web browser, connect to the Internet, and display the relevant page of Microsoft's Web site.

1. Click the Office Assistant, which displays several options:

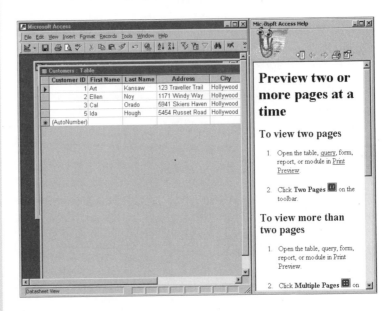

The Office Assistant's options relate to the tasks you recently completed. (If none of the options is helpful, you can type a question in the Search box and click the Search button to have the Office Assistant look up matching topics.)

2. Click the *Preview Two Or More Pages At A Time* option to display the Help window shown below. (If this option is not available, click any option, just to see how Help works.)

3. Read the Help topic and then close the Help window.

Now let's search Help's index:

More about the Office Assistant

If the Office Assistant displays a light bulb above its icon, it has a tip for you. Click the light bulb to see the tip. To move the Office Assistant to another location on the screen, simply drag it. If having the Office Assistant on the screen bothers you or if you want to customize it, click the Office Assistant's Options button to open the Office Assistant dialog box. Here you can select and deselect various options that control when the Office Assistant appears, whether it makes sounds, and what tips it displays. To turn off the Office Assistant, deselect the Use The Office Assistant check box. (To make the Office Assistant temporarily disappear or reappear, choose Hide/Show The Office Assistant from the Help menu.) On the Gallery tab, you can click the Back or Next buttons to scroll through the animated characters available for the assistant (the default is the paper clip) and then click OK to change the assistant. (You may need to insert the installation CD-ROM to complete the switch.)

1. Click the Microsoft Access Help button on the toolbar, and then click one of the displayed options to open the Help window on the right side of your screen.

The Microsoft Access Help button

2. On the Help window's toolbar, click the Show button and then click the Index tab, which looks like this:

The Show button

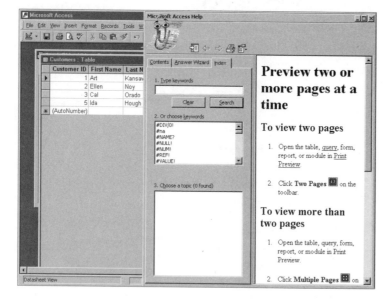

3. In the Type Keywords box, type *print*. The list below scrolls to display topics beginning with the letters you type.

4. Click Search, scroll the list of topics, and click *Print a Help topic*. Help displays that topic in the pane on the right.

5. Click the Close button.

Ending an Access Session

That's a lot of work for one chapter, and you might be ready for a break. When you finish working with Access, simply quit because the data is already saved. Let's quit Access now:

1. Click the Close button at the right end of the Access title bar (not the Table window's title bar).

2. If the Office Assistant asks whether you want to save your changes to the design of the table, click Yes.

Other ways to quit

Here are some other ways to quit Access:

- Choose Exit from the File menu.
- Press Alt, press F (the underlined letter in *File* on the menu bar), and then press X (the underlined letter in *Exit* on the File menu).
- Double-click the Control menu icon—the key—at the left end of the Access title bar.

2

Tables and Forms

You customize a table's structure, including setting field properties to control what data can be entered and how it looks. Then you see how to use forms to enter and review data. Finally, you customize a form in design view by editing and adding various components.

The methods for editing table structure and entering data covered in this chapter can be applied to any table you create. You can then maintain efficiency and ensure the accuracy of your work.

Table and form created and concepts covered:

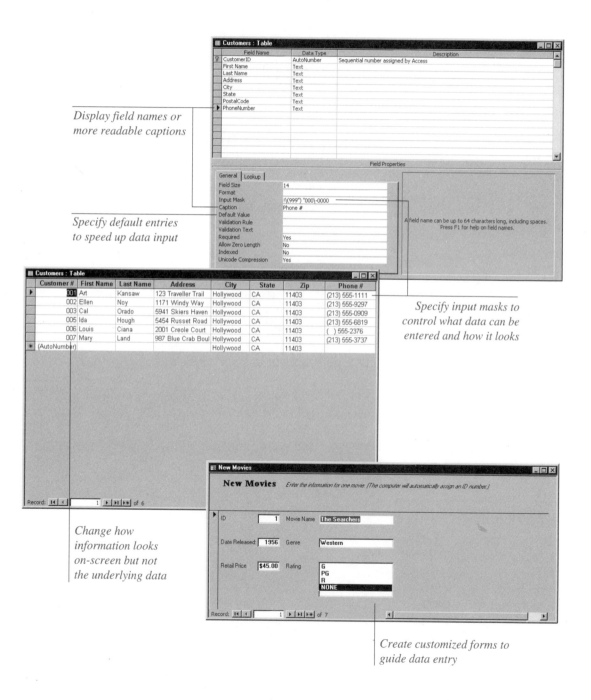

Display field names or more readable captions

Specify default entries to speed up data input

Specify input masks to control what data can be entered and how it looks

Change how information looks on-screen but not the underlying data

Create customized forms to guide data entry

I n Chapter 1, you learned how to create a database table using the Table Wizard and how to enter and edit records. You saw that tables created this way come with a predetermined structure that controls the kind of data you can enter and the way it looks in the table. In this chapter, you go behind the scenes to examine the table's structure more closely. We show you how to change the structure and how to give the tables you create from scratch the appropriate structure. Also in this chapter, you'll take a look at forms, which can greatly facilitate data input.

Editing Table Structure

When you used the Table Wizard to set up the Customers table, the wizard made several decisions about the table's design. But those decisions aren't cast in stone. Let's examine the structure of the Customers table and see how to change it:

1. Start Access and open the database you created in Chapter 1 by double-clicking South Ridge Video in the list of existing databases at the bottom of the Microsoft Access dialog box.

2. With the Tables list displayed and Customers selected in the Database window, click the Open button. Access opens the Customers table in its own window.

The View button

3. Click the View button on the toolbar to switch to design view. (See the tip below.) Access shows your table's structure like this:

Switching views

The View button is a toggle that switches between datasheet and design views. Its icon changes depending on which view is active. If you find that toggling is too confusing, you can click the arrow to the right of the button and select the view you want from a list.

As you can see, in design view the Table window is divided into two sections. The top half lists the table's field names, data types, and descriptions (if any). The bottom half lists the properties assigned to the field selected in the top half.

About Data Types

The data type of a field determines what kind of information you can put in the field and how Access can work with the information. We won't spend much time discussing the Access data types now, but we'll introduce the concept here, give you a list of the available types, and leave it to you to explore the different types as you need them, using the Help feature. Follow these steps to take a look at the types used in this table:

1. First press Enter to move to the Data Type column for the CustomerID field.

2. Click the column's arrow button to drop down this list of types:

Selecting a data type

3. You don't need to change the type, so with AutoNumber highlighted in the list, press Enter to move to the Description column.

4. Type *Sequential number assigned by Access* as this field's description and then press Enter to move to the next field. (This description will appear in the status bar when the CustomerID field is active in datasheet view.)

Adding field descriptions

For reference, turn the page for a description of each data type.

Data type definitions ————————————►

Data Type	Description
Text	General purpose data. Can contain letters, numbers, and other characters such as &, %, =, and ?. Can have up to 255 characters.
Memo	Similar to text, except that size limit is 65,535 characters.
Number	Numeric values that can be assigned the following field sizes: *Byte:* Whole numbers between 0 and 255. *Integer:* Whole numbers between −32,768 and 32,767. *Long Integer:* Whole numbers between −2,147,483,648 and 2,147,483,647. *Single:* Single-precision floating-point numbers between −3.402823E38 and −1.401298E−45, and between 1.401298E−45 and 3.402823E38. *Double:* Double-precision floating-point numbers between −1.79769313486231E308 and −4.94065645841247E−324, and between 1.79769313486231E308 and 4.94065645841247E−324. *Replication ID:* Globally unique identifier (GUID).
Date/Time	Valid dates are from January 1, 100 to December 31, 9999, including leap years. Can show dates, times, or both. Can have a variety of formats.
Currency	Numeric values formatted with up to 4 digits to the right of the decimal point and up to 15 to the left. Currency data typically shows negative values in parentheses and has money formatting. Can also be used for fixed-point calculations on numeric values.
AutoNumber	A unique sequential or random numeric value automatically assigned by Access to each new record in the table. Can be assigned a field size of Long Integer or Replication ID. Can be used as the primary-key field for tables in which none of the fields have a unique set of values. Cannot be updated.
Yes/No	Used for data that has only two possible values, such as yes/no or on/off.
OLE Object	Can hold a graphic or other object (spreadsheet, sound, video) created with Windows OLE-supporting applications. The object can either be linked to the field or embedded in the field.

Restructure warning

When restructuring a table, bear in mind that some data types cannot be converted to other types without loss of data. Adding a new primary key may result in errors, and reducing field sizes may result in data loss. If you attempt a restructure that will result in corrupted or lost data, Access advises you of the problem and gives you the choice of continuing or canceling the restructure.

Data Type	Description
Hyperlink	Can be a path to a file on your hard drive, a UNC path to a file on your network server, or a URL to an object on the Internet or an intranet. Access moves to the appropriate destination when you click a hyperlink.
Lookup Wizard	Not a data type. Used to create a field that allows you to look up a value in a different table or select one from a list. See page 42 for an example.

Using Field Properties

Field properties refine field definitions in various ways, and the available properties change depending on the field's data type. You will use some properties frequently, others rarely. In this section, you'll explore the more common properties.

Setting the Field Size

You can set a field size for the text and number data types. For text fields, the size indicates the maximum number of characters you can enter in the field. Up to 255 characters are allowed. If you try to enter, paste, or import a field value that is longer than the specified size, Access truncates the data.

Text field size

Let's set the size of the text fields of the Customers table:

1. In the field grid, click anywhere in the State field to display its properties in the Field Properties section.

2. Double-click 20 in the Field Size edit box to select it, and type 2. Now you can enter no more than two characters, such as the two-letter codes used for US states.

3. Repeat steps 1 and 2 to assign the following field sizes:

Field	Size	Field	Size
First Name	10	City	25
Last Name	12	PostalCode	10
Address	25	PhoneNumber	14

The Field Size property for number fields is different from that of text fields. A number field's size is determined by the complexity of the format selected (see the table on the facing page). You'll see how to set the size of number fields later, when you create a different table.

Number field size

Setting the Format

You use the Format property to specify how the characters entered in a field will appear on the screen. Depending on the data type, you may be able to select one of several predefined formats. You can also specify custom formats. Let's tell Access to always display three digits in the CustomerID field:

1. Click anywhere in the CustomerID field and then click the Format edit box in the Field Properties section.

Predefined formats →

2. Click the arrow to view a list of predefined formats for the AutoFormat data type. Then press Esc to close the list.

Custom formats →

3. Type *000* to tell Access to enter three digits, using leading zeros unless you enter something else. Now if the CustomerID is *3*, Access will display the entry as *003*:

Specifying an Input Mask

To control the display of data, you can also specify an *input mask*, or character pattern, that determines how data looks on the screen and what kind of data can be entered in the field. When you used the Table Wizard to set up the Customers table, Access specified input masks for two fields. Let's take a look at them and make some changes:

The zip code input mask →

1. Click anywhere in the PostalCode field in the field grid to display these field properties:

In the Input Mask edit box, the 0s are placeholders for digits you must enter and the 9s are placeholders for optional digits—in this case, a zip-code extension. The backslash followed by a hyphen indicates that Access will enter the hyphen, whether or not you enter the extension.

Required and optional digits

2. You are not using zip-code extensions in the Customers table, so click an insertion point to the right of the last 9, and press Backspace six times to delete all but the five zeros. Access will now accept only five digits in this field, even though the field size is larger.

3. Set the Field Size property to 5 to match the input mask.

4. Now click anywhere in the PhoneNumber field to see this more complicated input mask:

The phone number input mask

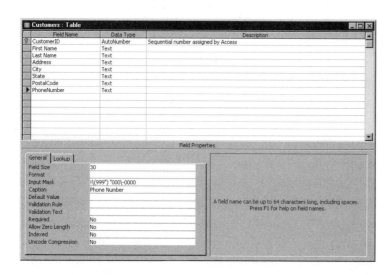

Again the 0s are required digits, and the 9s are optional digits or spaces. Backslashes precede characters that Access will insert. (The program will also insert the characters enclosed in quotation marks.) The exclamation point tells Access to right-align the characters you enter.

5. Leave this input mask as it is. Because you have already entered optional area codes for all the phone numbers in the table, you don't want to introduce inconsistency by deleting this part of the mask.

The Input Mask Wizard

If you install the Advanced Wizards, you can use the Input Mask Wizard to create a mask. Click the Build button at the right end of the Input Mask edit box (the one labeled with …) to have the wizard walk you through the necessary steps. You can preview predefined lists of masks or click Edit List to create your own mask templates using the characters described on page 38.

Here is a list of some characters used in the Input Mask edit box, together with what they mean to Access:

Input mask characters →

Character	Access's Action
#	Allows any digit, plus and minus signs, and spaces
L	Requires a letter
?	Allows any or no letter
A	Requires a letter or digit
a	Allows any or no letter or digit
&	Requires a character or space
C	Allows any or no character or space
<	Converts all following letters to lowercase
>	Converts all following letters to uppercase
\	Inserts the following character as entered
!	Right-aligns the entry

Let's use some of these to enter a couple of new input masks:

1. Click the First Name field in the field grid. In the Input Mask edit box, type >L<*????????* (with nine question marks) to tell Access to allow up to ten letters and to ensure that the first letter is capitalized.

2. Click the Last Name field and enter >L<*??????????* (with eleven question marks) as the input mask.

Assigning a Caption

By using the Caption property, you can substitute text for the field name when you display the table. The caption may simply repeat the field name with spaces added for readability, or it may display something different. Let's change a few of the captions specified by the Table Wizard when you created the table:

Spaces in field names

In Access, field names can have spaces (see page 13, where you renamed a field as First Name). However, many database programs do not allow spaces in field names. If you might need to export a database to a different program, you may want to assign names with no spaces to the fields and then add spaces in the captions so that the names will be more readable in tables, forms, queries, and reports.

1. Click anywhere in the CustomerID field to display its properties in the Field Properties section.

2. In the Caption edit box, click an insertion point to the right of the *D* in *Customer ID*, press the Backspace key twice to delete *ID*, and type #.

3. Repeat steps 1 and 2 to change the following captions:

Postal Code to *Zip*
Phone Number to *Phone #*

When you display the table, the new captions will be displayed as field names above their respective columns.

Setting a Default Value

The Default Value property lets you specify a field value that Access is to enter in the table automatically. Because the sample video store is small and most of the customers live in the same city, you can use this property for the City, State, and PostalCode fields to speed up data entry. Follow these steps:

1. Click anywhere in the City field to display its properties in the Field Properties section.

2. Click an insertion point in the Default Value edit box and then type *Hollywood* as the default city name.

3. Repeat steps 1 and 2 for the State field and the PostalCode field, specifying *CA* and *11403* as the default values.

Now every record you enter in the new database table will have Hollywood as its City field value, CA as its State field value, and 11403 as its PostalCode field value, unless you replace them with something else.

Requiring Entries

If you leave the table's field structure as it is, it would be possible to create incomplete customer records. To ensure that key information is always entered, you can specify that a field must have an entry. Try this:

1. Click the First Name field, click the Required edit box, click the arrow, and select Yes as this property's setting.

2. For all the other fields, double-click the Required edit box to change the entry from *No* to *Yes*.

Other Properties

Text, number, currency, and date/time fields can all be indexed. When a field is indexed, Access maintains behind-the-scenes lists of entries that allow it to process queries, searches, and sorts based on that field more quickly. (If a few values are repeated often, as is the case in the City, State, and PostalCode fields, then indexing the field doesn't save much processing

More about the Indexed property

To prevent duplicate values from being entered in a field that is not the table's primary-key field, you can set the Indexed property for that field to Yes (No Duplicates). Access automatically specifies this setting for the Indexed property of the primary-key field. To view or edit a table's indexes, you can switch to design view and click the Indexes button on the toolbar or choose Indexes from the View menu. Access lists the indexed fields in the Indexes window. Here, you can edit existing indexes, add new ones, or delete them. (Deleting a field from the Indexes window does not delete the field or its data from the table.) The Indexes window is best used for creating multiple-field indexes. For more information, check Access's Help feature.

time.) Data entry and editing may be slower with indexed fields because Access must maintain the index as well as the table.

You use the four remaining properties in the Field Properties section to check the validity of the data you enter in your tables. The Validation Rule and Validation Text properties are discussed in more detail on page 115. You will rarely need to use the Allow Zero Length property (available for text fields), and you don't set it for any of the fields in this table. Nor will you need to set Unicode Compression, which decreases the total storage size of the database.

Switching Back to the Table

Now let's return to the table to see the effects of your changes:

1. Click the View button on the toolbar. When Access asks if you want to save the table, click Yes. (The message appears as an Office Assistant "bubble" if the Assistant is visible, or in a dialog box if the Assistant is hidden or turned off. See the tip on page 28 if you want to hide the Office Assistant as we have.)

2. Two more dialog boxes may appear, one about lost data and the other about data integrity rules. Click Yes in both boxes.

The table reflects all the visual changes you made to its structure. The Customer # field displays three digits, and Hollywood, CA, and 11403 have been entered by default in the empty record at the bottom of the table. Let's add one more customer:

1. Move to the empty record at the bottom of the table and enter the data below in the indicated fields. (Try typing *louis* or *LOUIS* instead of *Louis* to see how Access responds.) Press Enter to skip the City, State, and Zip fields. To skip the phone number's area code, click the phone number field and then use the arrow keys to position the insertion point to the right of the closed parenthesis. Press Enter again to complete the record.

Skipping entries

First Name	Last Name	Address	City	State	Zip	Phone #
Louis	Ciana	2001 Creole Court				5552376

Here are the results:

Customer #	First Name	Last Name	Address	City	State	Zip	Phone #
001	Art	Kansaw	123 Traveller Trail	Hollywood	CA	11403	(213) 555-1111
002	Ellen	Noy	1171 Windy Way	Hollywood	CA	11403	(213) 555-9297
003	Cal	Orado	5941 Skiers Haven	Hollywood	CA	11403	(213) 555-0909
005	Ida	Hough	5454 Russet Road	Hollywood	CA	11403	(213) 555-6819
006	Louis	Ciana	2001 Creole Court	Hollywood	CA	11403	( ) 555-2376
(AutoNumber)				Hollywood	CA	11403	

Creating Tables from Scratch

Although it's often faster to use the Table Wizard to create tables, you need to know how to set up tables on your own for those times when the Access templates don't quite fit the bill. Let's create a table to hold movie information:

1. Close the Customers table, saving any layout changes.

2. With the Tables icon selected in the Database window, double-click Create Table In Design View. Access displays an empty Table window in design view with the insertion point blinking in the first field.

Starting a new table

3. Type *Movie Name* in the first field and press Enter to move to the Data Type column, where Access suggests Text as the data type. Access has also created some default settings in the Field Properties section.

4. Press Enter twice to accept Text as the data type, skip the Description column, and jump to the next field.

5. Name this field *Date Released*, set its data type to Number, click the Field Size edit box, click the arrow button, and set this property to Integer.

6. Now create these fields:

Field Name	Data Type	Properties
Rating	Text	Field Size = 4
Retail Price	Currency	
Genre	Text	

Since you know that there are only a few ratings to choose from, you can use the Lookup Wizard to create an edit box with a drop-down list that defines all the possible values for

Combo boxes ──────────►

The Lookup Wizard ──────────►

the Rating field. Here are the steps for creating this element, which is called a *combo box:*

1. Click the Data Type column for the Rating field, click the arrow button, and select Lookup Wizard to display this dialog box:

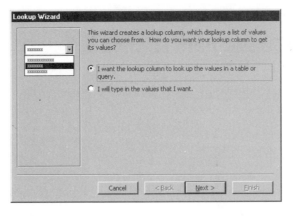

2. Select the option that allows you to type in values and click Next to display this dialog box:

3. Leave Number Of Columns set to 1 and press Tab to move to the empty field in Col1.

4. Enter *G* and press Tab. Then enter *PG, R,* and *NONE*, pressing Tab to move to a new field for each rating. Click Next.

5. Leaving the lookup name as Rating, click Finish.

6. In the Field Properties section, click the Lookup tab to display the properties shown on the facing page.

Looking up values in a table

When all the possible values for a field are listed as unique entries in an existing table or query, you can have Access refer to that table whenever you need to select the field value. See page 100 for an example of this.

7. Because you want to limit the data in this field to the entries in the lookup list, click the Limit To List edit box and change this property to Yes.

Now let's see how this table looks in datasheet view:

1. Click the View button on the toolbar, click Yes to save the table, and assign *Movies* as its title.

Saving the table

2. When asked whether you want to create a primary key, click Yes. Access adds an ID field and displays an empty record in datasheet view, ready for you to enter data.

3. Press Enter, type *The Searchers*, press Enter again, type *1956*, and press Enter.

4. In the Rating field, click the arrow button, select NONE from the list, and press Enter.

5. Type *45* as the price, press Enter, type *Western*, and press Enter to end the record. With column widths adjusted, the table looks like this:

6. Close the table window, saving your layout changes.

Now let's build up your database with another table so that you have something to work with later:

1. Create a new table in design view with the following fields:

Field Name	Data Type	Properties
Rental Terms	Text	
Days	Number	Field Size = Byte
Cost	Currency	
Daily Fine	Currency	

2. Click the View button on the toolbar, save the table as *Terms*, and click No when asked whether you want to create a primary key.

3. Then insert the following data in the table:

Rental Terms	Days	Cost	Daily Fine
New Release	1	3.5	10
Oldie Weekend	3	2	5
One Day Oldie	1	1	5

4. Close the Table window.

Using Forms to Enter and View Data

By now you are familiar with the procedure for entering data directly in tables, but with many databases it's easier to use forms to input data because they are more intuitive. As a demonstration, we'll create some very simple forms in this chapter. We'll tackle more complex forms in Chapter 5.

Creating AutoForms

For your first form, you'll create an input screen for the Customers table. Follow these steps:

The New Object button

1. Select Customers in the Tables list of the Database window, click the arrow to the right of the New Object button on the toolbar and then click AutoForm. (You could just click the New Object button, but we wanted you to see the list of available objects.) Access generates a form with all of the fields listed in the Customers table and displays the first record from the table, as shown at the top of the facing page.

2. Click the New Record button at the bottom of the Form window to move to an empty record.

3. With AutoNumber highlighted in the Customer # field, press Enter. Then type the following information, pressing Enter to move from one edit box to another:

First Name	Last Name	Address	City	State	Zip	Phone #
Mary	Land	987 Blue Crab Boulevard				2135553737

4. After you have entered the information, close the form by clicking the window's Close button, and when prompted, save the form as *New Customers*.

Using the Form Wizard

Now let's use a different method to create a form for entering movie information:

1. In the Database window, click the Forms icon to see the New Customers form you just created.

2. Click the New button. Access displays this dialog box:

Other autoforms and wizards

In addition to using the Form Wizard, you can create new forms directly in design view. You can also select one of three types of autoforms: Columnar displays fields one above the other from top to bottom, as in the New Customers form you just created; Tabular displays fields from left to right across the form; and Datasheet creates a form with rows and columns like a table. You can also create a form with the Chart Wizard (see page 142) or with the PivotTable Wizard (see the tip on page 149).

3. Notice that clicking the New button gives you more options than are available in the Database window (see the tip on the previous page for more information). Select Form Wizard and click OK to display this dialog box, where you select the table on which you want to base the form and the specific fields you want to include:

The Form Wizard →

4. Click the arrow to the right of the Tables/Queries edit box and select Table: Movies from the drop-down list. All of the fields in the Movies table are now listed in the Available Fields box.

5. Click the >> button to move all the fields to the Selected Fields box, and then click Next to display the next dialog box:

Quick finish

Having selected the table and fields in the first Form Wizard dialog box, you can click the Finish button to accept the default settings in the three remaining dialog boxes and jump directly to the new form's window.

6. Select each layout option to explore what's available, and then select Columnar and click Next. The dialog box shown on the facing page appears.

7. Select each style in the list box to see the choices available for the form's background. Then select Standard and click Next to display this dialog box:

8. Assign *New Movies* as the form's title. With the Open The Form To View Or Enter Information option selected, click Finish to display your new form, which looks like this:

Notice that, because you defined the possible entries for the Rating field using the Lookup Wizard (see page 42), Access automatically displays an arrow button for this field.

Customizing Forms

You have just created a new form, but suppose you want the form to look and act differently than the way Access has set it up. In this section, we demonstrate how to edit the New Movies form to meet your needs. As you follow these steps, save your work often by clicking the Save button, in case of computer crashes or power "hiccups":

The Save button

1. Click the View button on the toolbar to switch to design view. Then click the Maximize button on the Form window's title bar to expand the window to fill the screen, like this:

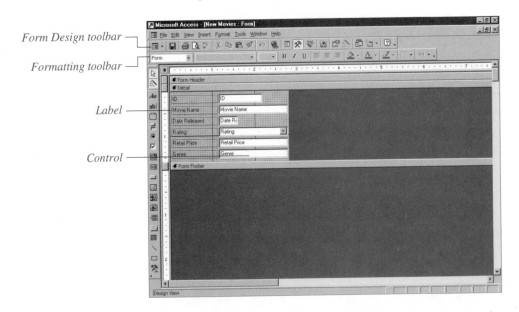

Form Design toolbar

Formatting toolbar

Label

Control

The Toolbox button

2. Whether your Toolbox toolbar is floating or docked as ours is, click the Toolbox button on the Form Design toolbar to turn it off. (You will use some of these tools later, but you don't need them right now.)

In design view, the Form window is divided into three sections. The Form Header can contain information such as a title that you want to have appear at the top of the form (it's currently blank). For each of the fields you selected for inclusion in the form, the Detail section displays a white box called a *control* where you will enter information in the new form. Each control is accompanied by a gray box called a *label* that contains the field's name or caption. The Form Footer functions like the Form Header. Two other sections, Page Header and Page Footer, are not visible in the form now on the screen. They can contain elements you want to appear on every page of a multi-page form. The window also displays horizontal and vertical rulers and gridlines that help you position controls and labels on the form.

Controls and labels

Moving Controls and Labels

Let's try rearranging some of the controls and their labels:

1. In the Detail section, move the mouse pointer to the right border of the active gridlined area, where the pointer changes to a bar with opposing arrows. Hold down the left mouse button and drag to the right, releasing the button when the active area just fills the form window. (Don't drag so far that the label boxes disappear from view.)

Sizing the active area

2. Click the Movie Name control. Small squares called *handles* appear around the control's border, like this:

Selecting controls

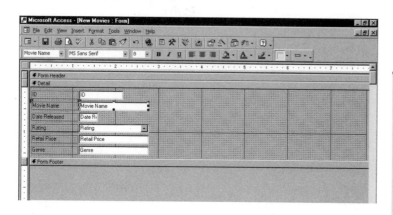

Two types of hands

To move a control and its label on a form so that they maintain their relative positions, select the control, point to the control's border, and drag the black open hand that appears. To move a control independently of its label, select the control, point to the large handle in the control's top left corner, and drag the black pointing hand that appears. Similarly, to move a label independently, select the label and drag the black pointing hand.

3. Point to the border (not a handle) of the selected control. When the pointer changes to a black open hand, hold down the left mouse button and drag the control and its label up and to the right of the ID control. (You can use the gridlines and rulers to help align the controls.)

4. Now select and drag the Genre control and its label to the right of the Date Released control.

5. Finally select and drag the Rating control and its label to the right of the Retail Price control. The form now looks like this:

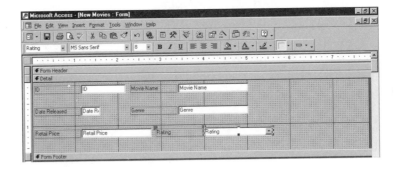

Sizing Controls and Labels

You may have noticed that several of the label boxes and control boxes are too big for their contents. Let's change the sizes now:

1. Select the Date Released label and point to the middle handle on the right side. When the pointer changes to a double-headed arrow, hold down the left mouse button and drag to the left until the label is just big enough to display its text.

2. Make the boxes for the ID and Retail Price labels the same size as for the Date Released label.

3. Now adjust the size of the boxes for the ID and Retail Price controls to match the size of the Date Released control. (It's OK that you can't see all of *Date Released* and *Retail Price*. The actual data will fit in the control boxes, even though the field names don't.)

4. Select the box for the ID control, and point to the large handle in the top left corner. When the pointer changes to a pointing hand, hold down the left mouse button and drag to the left, moving the control box until it is next to the ID label.

5. Size and rearrange the remaining labels and controls until your form looks like the one shown on the facing page.

Aligning controls

You can use the Align command on the Format menu to left-align, right-align, top-align, or bottom-align the controls in your forms. First select the controls you want to align. Then choose Align from the Format menu and one of the commands from the submenu. You can also align the controls to the nearest gridline by choosing Align and then To Grid. To align the text within a control or label, select the control or label and click one of the alignment buttons on the Formatting toolbar.

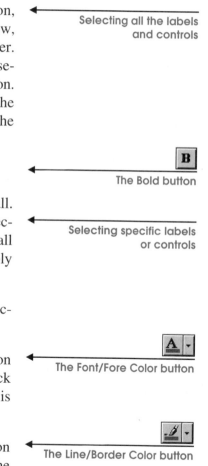

Making Information Stand Out

Now let's change the appearance of the controls:

1. Point to the top of the ruler to the left of the Detail section, and when the pointer changes to a black right-pointing arrow, hold down the left mouse button and drag down the ruler. When all the labels and controls are contained within the selection area defined by the pointer, release the mouse button. (You can also choose Select All from the Edit menu.) All the labels and control boxes are now selected, as indicated by the handles surrounding them.

Selecting all the labels and controls

2. Click the Bold button on the Formatting toolbar.

The Bold button

3. Suppose you decide the labels shouldn't be bold after all. Click a blank area of the Detail section to remove the selection, click the ID label, hold down the Shift key, and click all the other labels to add them to the selection. Then simply click the Bold button to return the labels to regular style.

Selecting specific labels or controls

4. Click a blank area of the Detail section to remove the selection, and then select the Movie Name control.

5. Click the arrow to the right of the Font/Fore Color button on the Formatting toolbar to display a palette of colors, and click red in the third row. The text in the Movie Name control box is now red.

The Font/Fore Color button

6. Click the arrow to the right of the Line/Border Color button and select yellow from the drop-down palette to surround the Movie Name control with a yellow border.

The Line/Border Color button

Changing Formats

The Rating field has only four possible values, so it might be easier to display all of the ratings in a list box rather than a combo box. Let's go ahead and change it:

List boxes

1. Select the Rating control and choose Change To and then List Box from the expanded Format menu.

2. Click the View button to see all the possible choices displayed in the new list box. Then switch back to design view.

3. If you want, resize the list box so that it is just the size needed to display the choices.

Deleting and Adding Controls

When initially designing a form, you may include fields that you don't need (for example, fields with default values). Or you may leave out some fields and later decide to include them. As a demonstration, let's delete a field from the form and then add it again. Follow these steps:

1. Select the Date Released control and press Delete. Access removes the control and its label from the form.

2. Click the Field List button on the Form Design toolbar, click Date Released in the list of fields that appears, and drag the field to the space below the ID control, where it was before.

3. Close the Field List box, resize the label and control to fit, and make the control bold.

Adding a Title

The Form Header section is currently blank, but you can use this section for a title, like this:

1. In design view, point to the border between the Form Header and Detail sections. When the pointer changes to a double-headed arrow, drag the mouse down to open the Form Header section.

2. Choose Toolbox from the View menu to display the Toolbox toolbar and, if necessary, dock it.

Adding values to a list box

If you created your own list of lookup values, you can add more values to it—for example, you could add *PG13* and *NC17* to the movie rating choices. In the form's design view, right-click the list box and choose Properties from the shortcut menu. On the Data tab of the Properties dialog box, click an insertion point in the Row Source edit box. Type any new terms, enclosing each term in quotation marks and separating terms with semicolons (but no spaces). Then close the Properties dialog box and, if necessary, adjust the size of the list box. (Changes you make to the form using this method are not reflected on the Lookup tab of the Field Properties section of the Table window, where you originally created the lookup list.)

3. Click the Label button on the Toolbox toolbar and move the pointer into the Form Header section, where it becomes a cross hair with a large A next to it. Then click to position an insertion point, and type *New Movies*.

The Label button

4. Repeat step 3, this time inserting an instructional label to the right of New Movies that contains the following text:

Enter the information for one movie. (The computer will automatically assign an ID number.)

5. Now right-click the New Movies label, choose Properties from the shortcut menu, and if necessary, click the All tab to display these options:

Changing the font, font size, and font weight

Label: Label13	✕
Format	Data	Event	Other	All

Name	Label13
Caption	New Movies
Hyperlink Address	
Hyperlink SubAddress	
Visible	Yes
Display When	Always
Vertical	No
Left	0.25"
Top	0.2083"
Width	0.6667"
Height	0.1458"
Back Style	Transparent
Back Color	-2147483633

6. Scroll through the list to get an idea of the properties you can set. (They are also grouped by category on the four other tabs.)

7. Scroll to the Font Name property, click the edit box, click the arrow button, and select Times New Roman. Next change the Font Size property from 8 to 14. Then click the Font Weight edit box, click the arrow button, and select Heavy. Close the Properties dialog box.

8. Resize the New Movies label by double-clicking any of its handles.

Sizing labels to fit their text

9. Select the instructional label, click the Italic button on the Formatting toolbar, and then resize the label.

I
The Italic button

10. Now adjust the positions of the labels by dragging the large handle in the top left corner of each label. (You may have to turn off the Snap To Grid command on the Format menu to align the text of the labels.) Turn the page to see the results.

Changing the Input Order

When you move controls around on a form, you need to check that you can still move from field to field in a logical way. Follow these steps to check the form:

1. Click the View button on the toolbar to switch to form view, and then move to a new record.

2. Tab through the controls, and then enter the following data in the correct fields, pressing Enter when you have finished:

Movie Name	Date Released	Genre	Retail Price	Rating
Frankenstein	1993	Horror	45	R

Access still moves through the controls in the order in which the fields appear in the table, even though you have moved them on the form. It also jumps to the ID control even though the user cannot change this field. Follow the steps on the facing page to make the order more logical.

More about gridlines and the Grid commands

By default, Access displays gridlines to help align the controls and labels on your form. You can turn off the gridlines by choosing Grid from the expanded View menu. Regardless of whether the gridlines are on or off, you can use the Snap To Grid command on the Format menu. You can also choose the Align/To Grid command or the Size/To Grid command from the Format menu to position or size the controls and labels. If you don't see gridlines when the Grid command is active on the View menu, open the Properties dialog box for the entire form by double-clicking the box at the junction of the horizontal and vertical rulers. Then on the Format tab, check the Grid X and Grid Y values, which set the number of gridlines per inch. If the values are too large, the grid may be too fine to display. Try changing the values to 10 or 12.

1. Click the View button to switch back to design view. Then select the ID control and click the Properties button on the Form Design toolbar to see the Properties dialog box.

The Properties button

2. On the Other tab, change the Tab Stop property to No so that Access will skip the ID control as information is entered. Then close the Properties dialog box.

3. Next right-click the Date Released control and choose Properties. Click the Tab Index property, which controls the order in which controls are activated when you press Tab, and change its setting to 2.

4. With the Properties dialog box still open, select the Genre control and change its Tab Index property to 3. Then change Retail Price to 4, and Rating to 5 by clicking each control in turn and adjusting the Tab Index setting. (Be sure the title bar of the Properties dialog box reflects the control you selected.) Then close the Properties dialog box.

5. Switch back to form view and tab through the controls, which are now activated sequentially.

Now that you have created a usable custom form, let's enter some more movie data:

1. Move to a new record and enter the following films (and any others that you would like):

Movie Name	Date Released	Genre	Retail Price	Rating
Cinderella	1950	Family	45	G
Frankenstein	1931	Horror	65	NONE
Star Wars	1977	Action	25	PG
Casablanca	1942	Drama	35	NONE
Braveheart	1995	Drama	19.99	R

2. Close the form and save your changes. Then close Access.

Now that you have a solid grasp of creating tables and inputting data, we can show you how to manipulate the data to get useful information out of the database. In the next chapter, you'll look at queries, reports, and data access pages, and you'll learn how to use switchboards to move among database components.

3

Queries, Reports, Data Access Pages, and Switchboards

You learn techniques for extracting information from a database with the Find command, filters, queries, reports, and data access (Web) pages. We also show you how to create and customize a switchboard to help others easily find what they need.

You can easily apply the methods learned in this chapter to track down information in your own databases, such as addresses in a particular region or stocks with specific performance characteristics.

Components created and concepts covered:

Use a select query to extract records from a table

New Releases : Select Query

Movies
*
ID
Movie Name
Date Released
Rating

Field:	ID	Movie Name	Date Released	Rating	Retail Price	Genre
Table:	Movies	Movies	Movies	Movies	Movies	Movies
Sort:						
Show:	☑	☑	☑	☑	☑	
Criteria:			>=1950 And <1960			
or:						

Use a report to produce printouts of grouped and summarized data

Microsoft Access - [Movies]

File Edit View Tools Window Help

100% ▾ Close W ▾ ⊡ ⊡ ▾ ② ▾

Movies

Rating   NONE
Casablanca
Date Released   Retail Price   Genre
1942 $35.00   Drama
Cinderella

Customers - Microsoft Internet Explorer - [Working Offline]

File Edit View Favorites Tools Help

Back Forward Stop Refresh Home Search Favorites History Mail Print Edit

Address C:\My Documents\Customers.htm

CustomerID		1
First Name	Art
Last Name	Kansaw
Address	123 Traveller Trail
City	Hollywood
State	CA
PostalCode	11403
PhoneNumber	21355511

Customers 1 of 6

Use a data access page to view data on the Internet or an intranet

Main Switchboard

South Ridge Video

☐ Enter a new customer

☐ Enter a new movie

Use a switchboard for quick access to frequently used database components

A this stage, you have learned how to create a database and to input information using tables and forms. In this chapter, you look at ways of extracting information using the simple Find command and filtering tools, as well as more complex queries, reports, and data access pages. You also examine switchboards, which allow you to move among database components in an intuitive way.

Using Find and Filters

Using the Find command is the simplest way to find specific information that you know is in a database, and the Find button makes things even simpler. For example, to find the film Casablanca in the South Ridge Video database, follow these steps:

1. If necessary, start Access and open the South Ridge Video database.

2. From the Tables list, open the Movies table.

The Find button

3. Click the Find button on the toolbar to display this dialog box:

Find and Replace	? X
Find	Replace
Find What:	Find Next
	Cancel
Look In:	ID
Match:	Whole Field	More >>

4. Type *Casablanca* in the Find What edit box, change the entry in the Look In drop-down list from *ID* to *Movies: Table* so that Access will search all fields, and click Find Next. Access highlights Casablanca in the table. (To see the result, you may need to move the Find dialog box by dragging its title bar.)

Moving dialog boxes

If you are not sure of the exact title of the movie, you can also use the Find button to find parts of an entry, like this:

Finding part of a field value

1. Replace Casablanca with *heart* in the Find What box, change the Match setting to Any Part Of Field, and click Find Next. Access highlights the *heart* in *Braveheart*.

2. Take a few minutes to familiarize yourself with the options in the Find dialog box and experiment with this useful tool on your own. Then click the Close button to close the dialog box.

When dealing with a very large table, you can temporarily focus on a subset of records that have something in common by using *filters*. Follow these steps to see how filters work:

1. In the Movies table, double-click NONE in the Rating field of the Casablanca record. Then click the Filter By Selection button on the toolbar. Access displays only those films with NONE as their rating.

The Filter By Selection button

2. Click the Remove Filter button to redisplay all the records in the table.

The Remove Filter button

3. Now highlight only *195* in the Date Released field of the Cinderella record and then click the Filter By Selection button to see only the movies made in the '50s. Then click the Remove Filter button again to redisplay all the records.

Using Queries

Suppose Mitch Egan wants a list of all of the movies and their retail prices. He doesn't want the ID, Date Released, Rating, or Genre information. To give Mitch what he wants, you will need to use a query. Queries are more complex than filters, but they are by far the most flexible way to search a database. Access provides two types of queries: select queries can find and extract information from a database, and action queries can update or delete records. In this section, you'll look at simple select queries. In Chapter 5, we'll show you more complex queries, and in Chapter 6, we'll look at action queries.

Here are some examples of common select queries:

- A supervisor might want a list of the emergency contacts for all the employees in his or her department.

- A sales manager might want to see the records for sales over a certain dollar amount.

- A training instructor might want to identify classes for which too few or too many people have enrolled.

More about filters

Filter By Selection can be used in tables, forms, and queries. You can even use filters within filters by first using one criterion and then filtering the results using a second criterion. For example, in a longer movie list, you might want to find all the Westerns that were made in the '50s. If you can't easily select the criteria for filtering in the table, click the Filter By Form button on the toolbar to set up filters using drop-down lists.

- A purchasing officer might want a list of vendors who carry all the supplies needed for a particular job so that one order can be placed instead of several.

Access answers a select query by identifying the subset of records and fields that meet the query's criteria and placing the subset in a temporary table called a *query datasheet*.

Query datasheets

Selecting Specific Fields

Let's go ahead and create the query that asks for every movie and its retail price. Follow these steps:

1. Click the arrow to the right of the New Object button on the toolbar and select Query from the drop-down list.

2. When Access says you must save the Movies table before creating the query, click Yes. Access displays this dialog box:

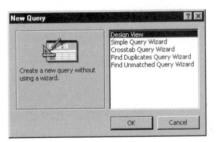

The Simple Query Wizard

3. Click Simple Query Wizard and then click OK. Access displays this dialog box:

Other query wizards

The other options in the New Query dialog box guide you through the process of creating different types of queries. We discuss crosstab queries in a separate tip on page 158. The Find Duplicates and Find Unmatched Query Wizards help you set up queries to find potential errors in the design of your database. You may want to explore these queries after reading Chapter 4.

4. Select Table: Movies from the Tables/Queries list, click Movie Name in the Available Fields list, and then click the > button to move it to the Selected Fields box. Repeat this step for Retail Price and click Next.

5. In the next dialog box, leave the Detail option selected and click Next.

6. Assign *Movie Prices* as the query's title and, with the Open The Query To View Information option checked, click Finish. Access runs the query and displays this Query window, which displays the results in a query:

Movie Name	Retail Price
The Searchers	$45.00
Frankenstein	$45.00
Cinderella	$45.00
Frankenstein	$65.00
Star Wars	$25.00
Casablanca	$35.00
Braveheart	$19.99
*	$0.00

Record: 1 of 7

7. If you want, you can print the query datasheet for Mitch Egan by clicking the Print button on the toolbar.

Printing query results

8. Click the Close button to close the Query window.

The Queries list in the Database window now includes Movie Prices as an existing query. Any time you want a list of movies and their prices, you can click the Queries icon on the objects bar, select this query, and click Open. Access will run the query again and display a new datasheet of results. If you have made changes to the Movies table, these changes will be reflected in the new datasheet.

Rerunning saved queries

Selecting Specific Records

You now know how to ask questions that require Access to select fields from a table. What if you want Access to select fields from specific records only? For example, suppose a customer wants a list of all the action films with a PG rating. Follow the steps on the next page to obtain this list.

Blocking entries in query datasheets

The query datasheet has an empty record at the bottom. An inexperienced user might add partial records to the table on which the query is based by making entries in this record. To avoid this kind of partial updating from a query, be sure that all of the table's fields require an entry (see page 39).

Creating new queries

1. In the Queries list, double-click Create Query In Design View to display this dialog box, where you specify the table you want to work with:

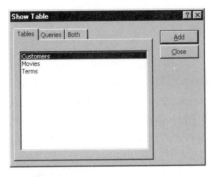

Specifying a table

2. On the Tables tab, select Movies, click Add, and click Close. You then see this Query window in design view:

In the top half of the window, a Movies box lists the fields in the Movies table. (The * at the top of the list represents all the fields.) Below is a table grid called the *query by example (QBE) grid*, in which you can visually construct the query.

Query by example (QBE) grid

Adding a field

3. In the Movies box, double-click the Movie Name field to tell Access to include Movie Name field values in the results of your query. Access transfers the Movie Name field to the first column of the QBE grid's Field row, identifies the field's table in the Table row, and displays a check mark in the box in the Show row to indicate that Movie Name field values will appear in the query datasheet.

4. Double-click Rating in the Movies box to transfer it to the second column of the QBE grid. Then scroll the Movies box

and double-click Genre. (If you double-click the wrong field name, press the Delete key to delete the highlighted entry, and then try again.)

5. With the Show boxes of these three fields selected, click the Run button on the toolbar. Here's the result:

The Run button

Movie Name	Rating	Genre
The Searchers	NONE	Western
Frankenstein	R	Horror
Cinderella	G	Family
Frankenstein	NONE	Horror
Star Wars	PG	Action
Casablanca	NONE	Drama
Braveheart	R	Drama

Record: 1 of 7

Most of these movies are not PG-rated action films, so you still have some work to do on this query. Follow these steps:

1. Click the View button on the toolbar to return to the Query window in design view.

Modifying queries

2. Click the Criteria row of the Rating column and type *pg*.

3. Then click the Criteria row of the Genre column, type *ACTION*, and click the Or field below to see the new query criteria:

Field:	Movie Name	Rating	Genre			
Table:	Movies	Movies	Movies			
Sort:						
Show:	☑	☑	☑	☐	☐	
Criteria:		"pg"	"ACTION"			
or:						

You are telling Access to select the records that have both the value PG in the Rating field and the value Action in the Genre field, and to display the values from the Movie Name, Rating, and Genre fields in the datasheet. Notice that the Criteria row

The Table row

When you are working with the fields from just one table, you don't need to display the Table row in the QBE grid. To turn it off, deselect Table Names from the expanded View menu.

is not case sensitive (you can use capital or lowercase letters), and that Access has enclosed the criteria in quotation marks.

Turning off field display

4. It's not really necessary to include the Rating and Genre values in the result of this query, so click the Show check boxes for these columns to remove their check marks.

5. Click the Run button. As you can see, Star Wars is the only movie that meets the query criteria.

6. Close the Query window, saving the query as *PG Action Movies* when prompted.

Using Wildcards

Suppose a customer wants to know if South Ridge Video has a particular movie. The customer can remember what the movie is about but not the movie's name, except that it begins with the letter *C*. You can search for all the movies beginning

The * wildcard

with *C* by using a query with the * wildcard, a placeholder that represents any character or characters. Let's create this query now:

1. From the Queries list of the Database window, create a new query using design view.

2. Add the Movies table to the Query window and then close the Show Table dialog box.

Adding all the fields

3. Double-click the title bar of the Movies box. All of the fields are highlighted.

4. Point to the selected fields, hold down the left mouse button, drag the pointer to the first column of the QBE grid, and release the mouse button. Access enters the fields in the columns of the grid in the order in which they appear in the table.

The Like operator

5. In the Criteria row of the Movie Name column, type *C** and press the Tab key to move to the next column. Access changes the criteria to *Like "C*"*. The * wildcard tells Access to look for a field value that starts with *C* and is followed by any number of additional characters. Because you are not looking for an exact match, Access clarifies the criteria by preceding it with the Like operator.

6. Run the query. Access displays this datasheet:

ID	Movie Name	Date Released	Rating	Retail Price	Genre
3	Cinderella	1950	G	$45.00	Family
6	Casablanca	1942	NONE	$35.00	Drama
(AutoNumber)		0		$0.00	

As you can see, the * wildcard is useful when you need to find records that are similar but not the same. You can place the * wildcard before, after, and between characters, and you can use it more than once in a single field. For example, you could have used the criterion *Like "C*B*"* in the Movie Name field to find only Casablanca.

In addition to *, you can use the ? wildcard as a placeholder for one character. For example, you could find Frankenstein by typing *Frank???????* in the Criteria row of the Movie Name column of a query.

Both the * and the ? wildcards can be used to locate records when you are unsure of the spelling of a field value, and the more information you can supply, the more specific the query datasheet will be. For example, there may be hundreds of movies beginning with *C* in a true movie database, but you could narrow the search for Casablanca by typing *C** as the Movie Name criterion and *Drama* as the Genre criterion.

Editing Query Datasheets

If you entered the information for the Movies table exactly as it is shown on page 55, the Movies table contains an error. Cinderella was made in 1950 and the Motion Picture Association of America did not begin rating films until 1966, so Cinderella should have a NONE rating. If you correct the record in the query datasheet that results from running the *Like "C*"* query, Access automatically corrects the record in the table. Follow the steps on the next page.

The ? wildcard

The OfficeLinks button

If you have Microsoft Office, it is simple to export the information in an Access table, query, or report for use in Word or Excel. Select the database component from the appropriate list in the Database window, click the arrow to the right of the OfficeLinks button on the toolbar, and select Publish It With MS Word or Analyze It With MS Excel from the drop-down list. The selected application opens with the table, query, or report loaded. You can also follow this procedure to use a table or query as a mail-merge data source, by clicking the arrow to the right of the OfficeLinks button, selecting Merge It With MS Word, and then following instructions.

1. Click the Rating field in the Cinderella record to display an arrow button.

2. Click the arrow button, select NONE from the drop-down list, and click a different record.

The Database Window button

3. Click the Database Window button on the toolbar, open the Movies table, and verify that the Cinderella record has been updated. Then close the table and choose the query from the Window menu to redisplay it.

Using Mathematical Operators

Access allows you to use mathematical operators in criteria, including = (equal to), < (less than), > (greater than), <= (less than or equal to), and >= (greater than or equal to). These operators are often used for such tasks as identifying customers whose orders fall within a certain range. Let's try using a mathematical operator with the Date Released field to find all the movies in stock that were made after 1990:

1. Switch to design view and delete the criterion in the Movie Name column.

2. In the Criteria row of the Date Released column, type *>1990*.

3. Run the query. Access displays a datasheet for the two movies that were made after 1990.

Saving queries

4. Click the Save button on the toolbar. Because you have not yet given this query a name, Access displays the Save As dialog box.

5. Save this query as *New Releases*.

Using Logical Operators

As you saw on page 63, you can narrow down the focus of a query by specifying criteria in more than one field of the QBE grid. Sometimes you might want to extract records that meet all of the specified criteria in all the fields (this *And* that), and sometimes you might want to extract records that meet any of the criteria (this *Or* that). Let's look at a few examples.

The And Operator

Suppose you want only the movies that were made in the '50s. You can't simply change the criterion from your previous query to >1950. Instead, you must construct a range by using the And operator. Follow these steps:

1. Switch to design view and change the criterion in the Date Released field to *>=1950 And <1960*. The QBE grid looks like this:

Using And in one field

2. Run the query. The New Releases datasheet shows only the two movies made in the '50s.

Now follow these steps to get a list of Westerns made in the '50s by using an additional criterion:

1. Switch back to design view, leave the criteria in the Date Released column as they are, and type *Western* in the Criteria row of the Genre column.

Using And with more than one field

2. Run the query. The Searchers is your movie.

The Or Operator

As you have seen, when you enter criteria in more than one column, Access assumes that you want to extract records that meet all the criteria in all the fields. Now suppose you have a movie-buff customer who wants to see a list of movies that are either Action or Horror. Follow these steps:

1. Switch back to design view and delete the criteria under Date Released. Then replace the Genre criterion with *Action Or Horror*.

Using Or in one field

2. Run the query to extract the three movies that meet the criteria from the Movies table.

You can also use the Or operator with more than one field by using the Or row. Try this:

Using Or with more than one field

1. Switch to design view and in the Or row of the Retail Price column, type *<40.*

2. Run the query. Now the datasheet shows all the movies that are either less than $40.00 or have a Genre value of Action or Horror.

The Not and Null Operators

You use the Not operator to identify the records that don't meet a specified criterion and the Null operator to identify the records that have no value in a specific field. For example, you can tell Access to identify all the movies in the Movies table that have a rating, like this:

1. Switch to design view and delete the criteria in the Retail Price and Genre columns.

2. In the Criteria row of the Rating column, type *Not none.* (Double negatives, which are not considered correct English, are acceptable in database queries.)

3. Run the query. The datasheet shows only movies that have a rating other than NONE.

Saving with a different name

4. To save this query with a different name, choose Save As from the File menu to display this dialog box:

Or rows

In the QBE grid, only one row is designated as the Or row. However, the Or operator is implied for all the rows below the Or row. If you need to use more Or criteria, enlarge the QBE grid by dragging the window's bottom border downward and then enter the criteria in successive rows.

5. Type *Rated Movies* in the Save Query 'New Releases' To edit box and click OK.

Sorting with Queries

A basic feature of databases is the ability to sort data so that you can look at it in different ways. For example, the Movies table is currently sorted in ascending order based on the primary-key ID field. On page 23, we briefly mentioned that you can sort databases using the Sort Ascending and Sort Descending buttons. However, to sort on more than one column using this method, you have to rearrange the columns. Using a query, you can sort the table based on any criteria. For example, suppose you want to list the movies alphabetically by genre. Follow these steps:

1. Switch to design view and choose Clear Grid from the expanded Edit menu to delete the fields from the QBE grid.

2. Double-click the Rating field in the Movies box to move the field onto the QBE grid, and then double-click Movie Name. (You may need to scroll to the left to see the fields on the QBE grid.)

3. Click the Sort row of the Rating column, click the arrow button, and select Ascending.

4. Repeat step 3 for the Movie Name field.

5. Run the query. The results are shown below:

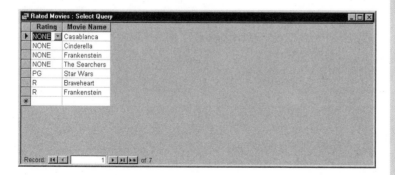

6. Close the Query window, clicking Yes to save your changes to the Rated Movies query.

With this introduction to queries under your belt, you are now equipped to carry out many of the queries commonly performed

Exporting tables, forms, queries, and reports

Information from an Access database is often used as part of a report created in another program, such as Word or Excel. To export the data in a table, form, query, or report for use in another program, choose Export from the File menu. Access then displays the Export dialog box, where you can select a file format from the Save As Type drop-down list, name the file, and click Export. If you select Text Files as the format, Access displays the Export Text Wizard, which helps you set up the text file exactly as you want it. If you select Microsoft Access as the format, you must specify in the File Name edit box the database to which you want to export the table, form, query, or report.

on databases. We'll pick up this topic later in Chapter 5, but for now, let's move on to another tool for extracting information: reports.

Using Reports

Creating a report is similar to creating a form. You can create one quickly by using the default autoreport, or you can use the Report Wizard to produce results more tailored to your needs. And when a specialized report is required, you can customize reports using many of the same techniques you use for forms.

Creating AutoReports

To start exploring reports, let's create an autoreport based on the Movies table:

1. Close all open windows except the Database window, and display the Tables list.

2. Select Movies in the list of tables, click the arrow to the right of the New Object button on the toolbar, and select Auto-Report from the drop-down list. After a few seconds, Access displays the report shown below. (We've scrolled the window so that you can see two full records.)

Saving a database object as another type

If you want to save an Access table, form, query, or report as a different kind of object, you can do so by first selecting the component you want from the appropriate list in the Database window and then choosing Save As from the File menu. Select the new object type from the Save As drop-down list, adjust the name if desired, and then click OK. You can then make adjustments to the new object in design view.

Because reports are usually created to produce printouts, Access displays the report in print preview so that you can see what it will look like on the page.

3. Click the Zoom button on the toolbar to zoom out for a bird's-eye view, like this:

The Zoom button

4. To see the second page of the report, click the Next Page button to the right of the page indicator in the bottom left corner of the Report window.

5. Now click the Zoom button again to zoom back in.

6. Click the Report window's Close button, and click No when asked whether you want to save the report.

Creating Reports with the Report Wizard

You probably noticed that the records in the report are in ID order. Suppose you want them organized by Rating order instead. To create a report that meets this need, you use the Report Wizard. Follow these steps:

1. In the Database window, click the Reports icon on the objects bar and then double-click Create Report By Using Wizard to display the dialog box shown on the next page.

Other autoreports and wizards

From the New Report dialog box, you can choose to create two types of autoreports: Columnar creates labels and controls running down the side of the report, and Tabular creates an autoreport with labels and controls running across the top. We explore the Chart Wizard on page 142 and describe the Label Wizard on page 80.

Selecting a table

Selecting fields

2. Select Table: Movies from the Tables/Queries drop-down list. In this report, you want to include all the fields from the Movies table except ID. Click >> to move all the fields to the Selected Fields box, select ID, and click < to remove it. Click Next to display the dialog box shown here:

Grouping report fields

3. To specify a grouping level, you designate a field or fields that are to be used as the basis for organizing and sorting the report. Select Movie Name and click >. The preview on the right shows that the report will now be grouped by the Movie Name field.

4. Select Rating and click >. The dialog box now looks like the one shown on the facing page.

5. Since you really want to organize the list of movies by rating, the report should be grouped by Rating first. To adjust the groupings, make sure the Rating field is selected in the preview window and click the up Priority arrow. After Rating and Movie Name switch places, click Next.

Changing the grouping order

6. Access asks whether you want to sort the remaining fields in a given order. This table is too small to take advantage of this option, but for larger databases you click arrows next to the edit boxes and select fields. In this case, simply click Next to display this dialog box:

Grouping by date or time

If you select a date field to group by when designing a report with the Report Wizard, you can click the Grouping Options button to group records by units of time from one minute up to a year. This can be useful when totaling sales for a month or quarter, or for almost any other time-dependent grouping of information.

7. Select the various options and watch the layout changes in the preview box on the left. When you've finished, select Outline 2 as the Layout option and Portrait as the Orientation option. Then click Next to move to the next dialog box.

8. Try out the different styles, and when you have previewed them all, select Corporate and click Next.

9. Access suggests Movies as the title for the report. Accept this default name, leave the Preview The Report option selected, and click Finish to display the report in print preview, as shown here (again, we've scrolled the window):

Changing sorting and grouping

Once you have assigned field groupings by using the Report Wizard, you can change how the fields are sorted and grouped by switching to design view and clicking the Sorting And Grouping button on the toolbar. In the window that appears, you can add new fields for grouping, change the sorting for each field (ascending or descending order), and change the grouping order. (To move a field up or down in the grouping order, click the field's row selector, point to the selector, hold down the left mouse button, and drag up or down.) In the Group Properties section, you can assign headers and footers to each group, group by each value or by a prefix, group by an interval or number of characters, and tell Access whether to keep groups together across page breaks.

Modifying the Report's Design

The Report Wizard greatly simplifies the process of creating reports, and you can always modify a report's design later if it doesn't quite meet your needs. (The techniques you use are similar to those used to modify forms, so if you skimmed

Chapter 2, you may want review the forms section.) Let's change the design of this report to enhance its appearance:

1. Switch to design view. If necessary, close the Toolbox toolbar and click the Maximize button on the Report window's title bar to expand the window like this:

This report is a good deal more complex than the forms you created in Chapter 2, but the major elements are the same. Controls placed in specific sections determine where the field values will be printed. The report's title, Movies, appears in the Report Header section and will be placed once at the beginning of the report. Rating has its own header, and the other fields have labels in the Movie Name Header section and controls in the Detail section. Also included are Footer sections for the page and for the report as a whole.

2. When fields are fairly obvious, labeling them creates needless clutter on a report, so select the Movie Name label (the box on the left) and press Delete.

<— **Deleting labels**

3. Now select the Movie Name control and point to its border. When the pointer changes to an open hand, drag the control to the left so that it aligns with the left end of the heavy line above, as shown on the next page.

4. Now click the Print Preview button on the Report Design toolbar to see what the report looks like.

The Movie Name section is now OK, but let's make the Detail section a little more presentable:

If at any time you want to change the entire format of a report or form, you can use an autoformat. Switch to design view and click the report or form selector (the small box at the junction of the horizontal and vertical rulers) to select the entire report or form. (The box will contain a black square bullet.) Then click the AutoFormat button on the toolbar. Access gives you the same choices of formatting you had when using the Report or Form Wizard, including font, color, and border combinations. You can also create your own custom autoformats so that if you spend time working out the best layout for a report or form, you can easily repeat it.

1. Switch to design view and click the Save button to safeguard the design changes you have made so far.

2. Now select all the labels in the Movie Name Header section (but not the Movie Name control) and all the controls in the Detail section. (Click one box, hold down the Shift key, and click each label and control to add it to the selection.)

3. Right-click any selected box, choose Properties from the shortcut menu, and click the All tab to display this dialog box, which lists all the properties used in reports:

4. Scroll to the Text Align property (towards the bottom of the All tab). Click the edit box, click the arrow button, and choose Center from the drop-down list. Close the Properties dialog box.

Aligning control and label text

5. Now move all of the selected labels and controls to the left to align with the Movie Name control.

6. Save the report and then click the Print Preview button to see how it is shaping up:

The Report Wizard added the gray boxes and blue lines to create visual structure in the report, but this formatting tends to clutter up the page. Let's trim it down a little bit:

1. Click Close on the Print Preview toolbar, and then enlarge the Rating Header section. (Point to the bottom of the section, and when the pointer changes to a bar with opposing arrows, drag downward.)

2. Click the gray line below the Rating control to select it, press Delete, and then go ahead and shrink the Rating Header section again.

3. Next select the thick blue line at the top of the Movie Name Header section and press Delete.

The Toolbox

You may not use many of the tools on the Toolbox toolbar, but a tool exists for almost every object you might want to add to a form or report. For example, you can use these tools to add text boxes, labels, option buttons, check boxes, graphics, and page breaks. Check the Help feature for details on how to use these tools to customize your forms or reports.

Aligning lines

4. Now click the thin blue line above the controls in the Detail section. (It may be hard to spot at first, but look carefully.) When you have selected the line, hold down the Shift key and also select the Date Released control.

5. Choose Align and then Left from the Format menu to both move the line to the left and align it precisely with the Date Released control.

6. Now save and preview the report.

Not bad, but you could do a few more touch ups. The movie name should be bolder, and maybe you should have deleted the line between the Date Released, Retail Price, and Genre labels and their controls instead of the thick blue line between movies. Follow these steps to make these adjustments:

1. Close the Print Preview window, select the Movie Name control and click the Bold button. Then select the Date Released, Retail Price, and Genre labels and click the Bold button to turn off bold.

2. Point to the bottom of the Movie Name Header section. When the pointer changes to a double-headed arrow, hold down the left mouse button and drag upward, shrinking the size of the Movie Name Header section so that the labels just fit. (Access won't shrink the section beyond the bottom of the lowest label or control.)

3. Select the thin blue line in the Detail section and press Delete.

Now let's draw the thick blue line:

Drawing lines

1. On the toolbar, click the Toolbox button to turn on the Toolbox toolbar. (If necessary, dock the toolbar by double-clicking its title bar so that you have an unrestricted view of the three labels in the Movie Name Header section.)

The Line button

2. Click the Line button on the Toolbox toolbar, point to the top left corner of the Movie Name control, hold down the left mouse button and drag to the right until the line spans the three labels at the bottom of the section. When you release the mouse button, the line snaps into place.

3. With the line selected, click the arrow to the right of the Line/Border Width button on the Formatting toolbar and select 3 from the drop-down palette to make the line thicker.

The Line/Border Width button

4. Click the arrow to the right of the Line/Border Color button on the Formatting toolbar and select magenta.

5. Finally, click the Properties button on the Report Design toolbar, set the Border Style property to Sparse Dots, and close the Properties dialog box.

6. Click the Toolbox button on the Report Design toolbar to turn off the Toolbox toolbar, and then save and preview the report, which is shown here:

Reports can become very complex and can include a good deal of formatting. We can't cover every technique for manipulating the appearance of reports, but you might take a look at some of the reports included with the sample databases that come with Access. For information on how to create reports based on multiple tables, see the tip on page 125.

Creating Mailing Labels

Now we'll take a quick detour to demonstrate another Access wizard: the Label Wizard. Once you learn how to use this wizard, you'll wish all programs made creating labels this easy.

Adjusting lines

If you have difficulty drawing a straight line, use the Properties dialog box to fix the problem. The Height property indicates how far up or down a line slopes from its point of origin, not its length. To make the line straight, change the Height property to 0. To specify the exact length of a line, use the Width property. (Other types of controls also have Height and Width properties you can use to help with the precise placement or sizing of controls.)

Suppose South Ridge Video occasionally sends out promotions to all its customers. To save time, you want to create a mailing-label report that can be used to print a set of labels whenever they are needed. Follow these steps:

1. Close any open windows except the Database window, and with the Reports icon selected, click the New button.

The Label Wizard

2. In the New Report dialog box, select Label Wizard, select Customers from the Choose The Table Or Query drop-down list, and click OK. The Label Wizard displays its first dialog box.

3. If necessary, select English in the Unit of Measure section and select Avery from the Filler By Manufacturer drop-down list. You then see these options:

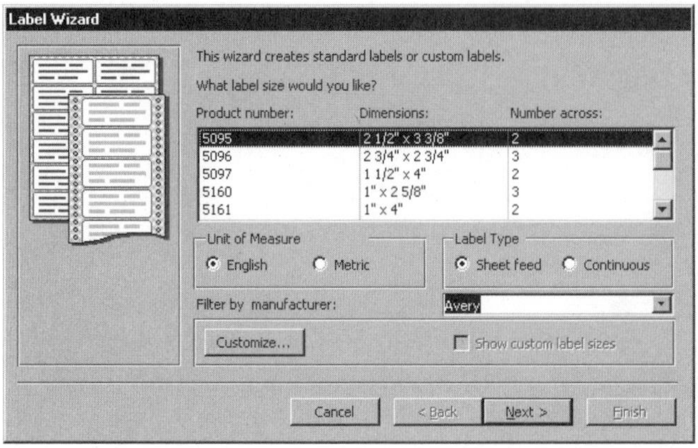

4. Choose a label type (we chose Avery 5160) and click Next to display the dialog box shown here:

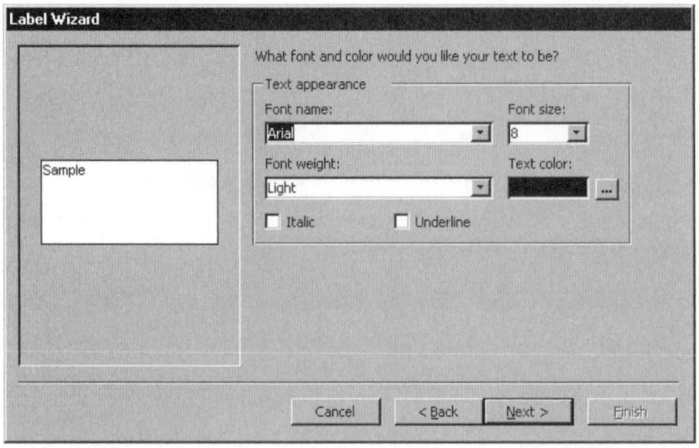

Using queries as a label source

You can use queries as the information source for labels. For example, to send information to customers in a specific sales area, you could create a query that extracts name and address information by city or zip code and then use the query datasheet as the basis for a mailing-label report. You could also create product labels (videos, disks, and so on) this way.

5. Change the font size to 10 and the font weight to Bold, and click Next to move to the dialog box shown here:

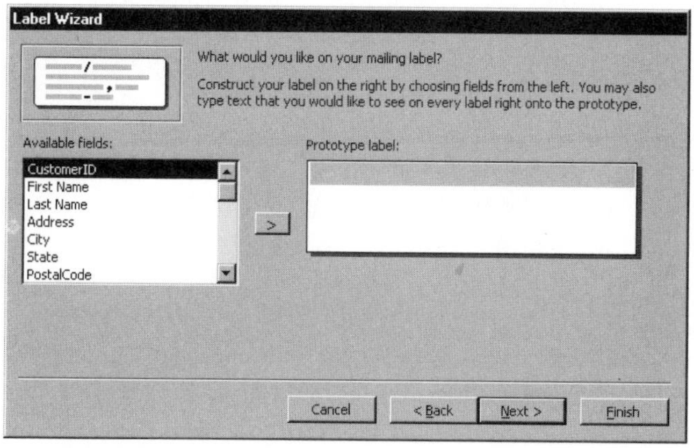

6. Double-click the First Name field to add it to the first line in the Prototype Label box. Press the Spacebar to insert a space, double-click the Last Name field to add it after the space, and press Enter to create a second line.

Adding fields

7. Double-click the Address field, and then press Enter to create a third line.

8. Double-click the City field, and type a comma and a space. Next, double-click the State field, press the Spacebar twice, and then double-click the PostalCode field to finish the third line. Click Next to display the dialog box shown below:

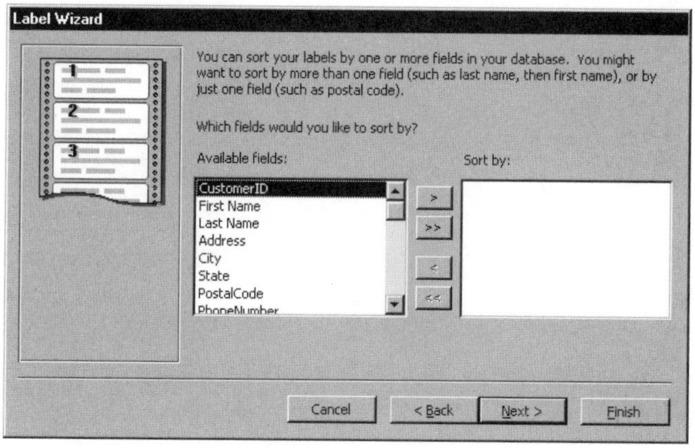

Label types

You will find almost all the Avery label formats listed in the Label Wizard's dialog box. If none of these label formats suit your needs, you can select a different brand from the Filter By Manufacturer drop-down list. You can also click the Customize button and in the dialog box that appears, click New. You can then specify the measurements of the label you want to use and save this new label for future use.

Sorting labels

Access allows you to sort the labels using any fields, even ones not included on the labels. For example, if you are doing a bulk mailing, you must sort by zip code.

9. To sort them by Last Name, double-click Last Name and then click Next.

10. Assign *Customer Mailing Labels* as the report's title and then click Finish. Access displays the labels in print preview, as shown here:

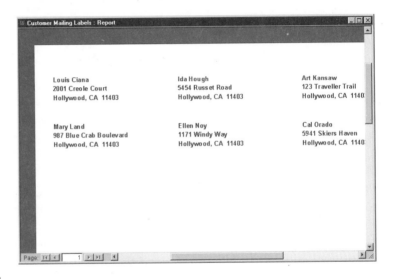

Printing Reports

You have looked at reports in print preview several times to get an idea of how they will look when printed. Using print preview can save a lot of time and paper. If the report is too wide or too long to fit neatly on a page, print preview shows the overflow pages and allows you to change the report's design or modify the page setup before you commit it to paper. (We have covered several ways to change the report's design in this section; we briefly discussed modifying the page setup on page 26.)

Access has already set all the page setup options to print the mailing labels you created in the previous section, so you don't need to make any changes for this report. You can go right ahead and give the printer some work to do:

Printing labels

Always print one test sheet of labels before sending an entire mailing-label report to your printer. To print just one page, choose Print from the File menu, select Pages in the Print Range section, type *1* in both the From and To boxes, and click OK. Then check the label alignment. If necessary, redo the mailing-label report by customizing the layout of your selected Avery label (see the tip on page 81) or by changing the font and font size. When you are sure the alignment is OK, print the entire mailing-label report.

1. Click the Print button on the Print Preview toolbar to accept all print defaults. Or if you want to make any changes to the default print settings, choose Print from the File menu, select the options you want, and click OK.

2. Then close the Report window.

   In this section, we have given you only a glimpse of the full potential of Access reports in the expectation that you will experiment with them as you use them. Remember, this experimentation has no effect on the structure of the underlying database tables or the data they contain.

Using Data Access Pages

Often people don't need to enter data into a database but do need to be able to check its information. If the database is available on a local computer or over a network, accessing it is no problem. But for people in distant locations, you can make information available over the Internet or an intranet with a feature called *data access pages*.

Data access pages are forms that are coded with HyperText Markup Language (HTML) so that they can be viewed using a Web browser such as Microsoft Internet Explorer. As a demonstration, follow these steps to convert an existing table to a data access page:

1. Select Customers in the Database window's Tables list.

2. Click the New Object button's arrow and select Page. This dialog box appears:

Creating data access pages from scratch

If you want to create a data access page from scratch, you can do so using design view or an Access wizard. Click the Pages icon on the objects bar, click the New button to display the New Data Access Page dialog box, click Design View, select the table or query you want to base the page on, and click OK. In design view, you can create a data access page using many of the same techniques you use to create forms. To add fields to the data access page, drag them from the Field List dialog box. You can use buttons on the Toolbox toolbar to add other objects to the page, and the buttons on the Alignment And Sizing toolbar to modify the alignment and sizing of controls and labels. When you finish, click the View button to switch to page view where you can get an idea of what your page will look like in a Web browser.

The Page Wizard →

3. Check that Customers is selected in the table list and then double-click Page Wizard.

4. In the wizard's first dialog box, click the >> button to move all the available fields to the Selected Fields box, and then click Next.

5. Click Next in the Page Wizard's second and third dialog boxes to accept the default selections.

6. With *Customers* specified as the title for the page, click the Open The Page option and click Finish. Access opens this data access page:

Using Web folders

A Web folder is a shortcut to a Web server where you can publish data access pages for viewing in Web browsers on the Internet or an intranet. To create a Web folder shortcut, start Windows Explorer, double-click Web Folders, and then double-click Add Web Folder to start the Add Web Folder Wizard. You can also create a Web folder from the Open or Save As dialog box by clicking Web Folders on the shortcuts bar and then clicking the Create New Folder button to start the Add Web Folder Wizard. The wizard then guides you through the process of entering a URL for the Web server. Once you have defined a Web folder shortcut, you can use it to save or open files. This feature works only if your Web server supports Web folders, so first check with your Webmaster or your Internet Service Provider.

Let's take a moment to get a feel for how the page works:

1. Click the record navigation buttons to move among the table's records.

2. Click the New Record button to display a record. Then type *Al* in the First Name box and *Laska* in the Last Name box.

3. Now click the Previous Record button. Access displays this message box:

The Required Entry property you set for the Address field in the table has carried over to the data access page.

4. Click OK to close the message box and then click the Undo Writing button on the page toolbar. You now see the information for the last record.

The Undo Writing button

Editing a Page

By default, Access lets you enter records into the database through a data access page. But most data access pages are meant to provide a way of viewing information in a database, not changing it. Let's make some changes to the new page:

1. Click the View button to switch to design view.

2. Right-click the Customer ID control and choose Properties from the shortcut menu to open the control's Properties dialog box.

3. On the Other tab, click the ReadOnly edit box, click its arrow button, and select True from the drop-down list. Leaving the Properties dialog box open, select each of the controls in turn and set their ReadOnly properties to True. Then close the Properties dialog box.

4. Click the View button to switch to page view.

5. Test your changes by trying to alter the record for Art Kansaw. Then click the New Record button and try to enter information.

6. Click the Undo Writing button to get out of the new record.

Having to click Undo Writing is a nuisance. Let's remove the New Record button from the page toolbar so that no one is tempted to try and add records through this page. While you're at it, you'll also remove other buttons that allow people to change the underlying table. Follow these steps:

1. Switch back to design view, scroll the window if necessary, select the toolbar in the Navigation section, and choose Properties from the View menu.

2. On the Other tab, change the ShowNewButton property to False to remove the New Record button from the toolbar.

3. Set the ShowDelButton, ShowSaveButton, and Show Undo-
   Button properties to False. Then close the Properties dialog box.

Saving data access pages

4. Click the Save button. Because data access pages are saved in
   their own files as well as a component of the database, Access
   displays the Save As Data Access Page dialog box. Type Customers as the filename and click Save to save the file in the
   My Documents folder.

5. Switch to page view, where your page looks like this:

6. Close the Data Access Page window, saving your changes
   when prompted.

   Now let's see how the new page looks when displayed by a
   Web browser (we're using Internet Explorer):

Previewing a data access
page in a Web browser

1. Start your Web browser. (You can work online or offline.)

2. Choose Open from the File menu to see this dialog box:

3. Click the Browse button and navigate to the My Documents
   folder, where Access has stored your Customers data access
   page as an HTML file. Select the file, click the Open button,
   and click OK. Your screen should now look like this:

Let's try a couple of ways to view information in the data access page:

1. First, minimize your Web browser's window, open the Customers table and add the following records:

First Name	Last Name	Address	City	Zip	Phone #
Al	Laska	1414 Icicle Lane	Beverly Hills	11210	3105559876
Montie	Anna	10000 Blue Highway	Beverly Hills	11210	3105558844

2. Close the Table window. Then activate your Web browser and click the Refresh button to reload the Customers data access page. (Notice that the record indicator now shows that the table has eight records.)

3. Move to the last record, select Beverly Hills, and click the Filter By Selection button on the page toolbar. The record indicator on the toolbar shows that two records meet this criterion.

4. Click the Next Record button to see the other record.

5. Now click the Remove Filter/Sort button.

6. Double-click the Last Name control and then click the Sort Ascending button.

7. Flip through the records to verify that the records are now sorted by last name.

8. Double-click the Customer ID control and then click Sort Ascending to restore the default order.

9. Close your browser's window.

That concludes our brief discussion of data access pages. You can explore data access page customization on your own as you get more comfortable with the program.

Using Switchboards

A switchboard allows you to quickly access the most commonly used parts of a database without having to understand what all the components are and how they relate to one another. To finish up this chapter, we'll show you how to create and customize a switchboard for the South Ridge Video database.

Creating a Simple Switchboard

At South Ridge Video, the most common tasks are entering new movies and entering new customers. Let's create a switchboard to quickly find those forms:

Setting the startup form

If you want to make a switchboard or any other form the first one seen when a database opens, choose Startup from the Tools menu and select the desired form name from the Display Form drop-down list. Other options in the Startup dialog box control whether toolbars can be customized, which shortcut menus are available, and whether the Database window and status bar are displayed. Any changes you make in this dialog box affect only the current database and will not take effect until you reopen the database or Access.

1. With any icon selected in the Database window, choose Database Utilities from the Tools menu and then Switchboard Manager from the expanded submenu.

2. Click Yes when asked whether you want to create a switchboard. You then see this Switchboard Manager dialog box:

The switchboard is divided into pages, and by default, Access creates a blank page. Let's add the two forms you have already created to it:

1. Click Edit to display this dialog box:

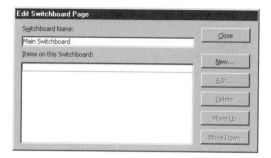

2. Click New to add an item to the Main Switchboard. Switchboard Manager displays this dialog box:

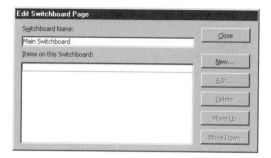

Adding forms to a switchboard page

3. Type *Enter a new customer* in the Text edit box and select Open Form In Add Mode from the Command drop-down list.

4. Select New Customers from the Form drop-down list and click OK to return to the Edit Switchboard Page dialog box, where *Enter a new customer* has been added to the list.

5. Click New again, type *Enter a new movie* in the Text edit box, select Open Form In Add Mode as the Command setting, and then select New Movies as the Form setting. Finally, click OK.

Now let's see what the switchboard looks like:

1. Close the Edit Switchboard Page and Switchboard Manager dialog boxes.

2. Click the Forms icon on the objects bar of the Database window. Then double-click Switchboard to display the window shown on the next page.

Taking a shortcut to a database

Not only can you make a database start with an easy-to-use switchboard, you can make opening a database much easier. Shrink the Access program window so that the Windows desktop is visible behind it, and then drag the switchboard form or any other database component out of the appropriate list in the Database window and onto the desktop as a shortcut icon. When you double-click the shortcut icon on the desktop, Access starts and the database is loaded with the selected component on the screen. To delete a shortcut icon, simply drag it to the Recycle Bin.

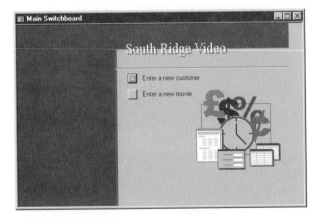

Customizing a Switchboard

You can modify the format of a switchboard in many ways. Most of the rules for moving controls and labels in forms and reports also apply to switchboards. Follow these steps:

1. Switch to design view, right-click the colored area to the left of the grid, choose Fill/Back Color, and select a new color. Then repeat this step for the colored area at the top of the grid.

2. Now choose Picture from the Insert menu. Navigate to the C:\Program Files\Microsoft Office\Office\Bitmaps\Dbwiz folder and double-click Resource. Then drag the graphic to the bottom right corner of the window.

3. Switch to form view to see these results:

4. Click each form button in turn and then close everything. When asked if you want to save your changes, click Yes.

TWO

BUILDING PROFICIENCY

In Part Two, you further develop the skills learned in Part One by adding more complex components to the database you created. In Chapter 4, we give you a set of guidelines for database design before showing you how to work with multiple tables. Then in Chapter 5, you create multi-table forms and multi-table queries. Finally, in Chapter 6, we show you how to use action queries to manipulate multiple records, and we suggest ways to manage your database efficiently and keep it secure.

4

Database Design

We give three basic rules for database design and introduce other tools that help you build less error-prone databases. Then we show you how to establish relationships so that you can work with multiple tables. We end the chapter with a discussion of data protection.

The guidelines given in this chapter can be applied to the design of any database, whether your organization buys or sells products or services, or manages people such as employees or students.

Components created and concepts covered:

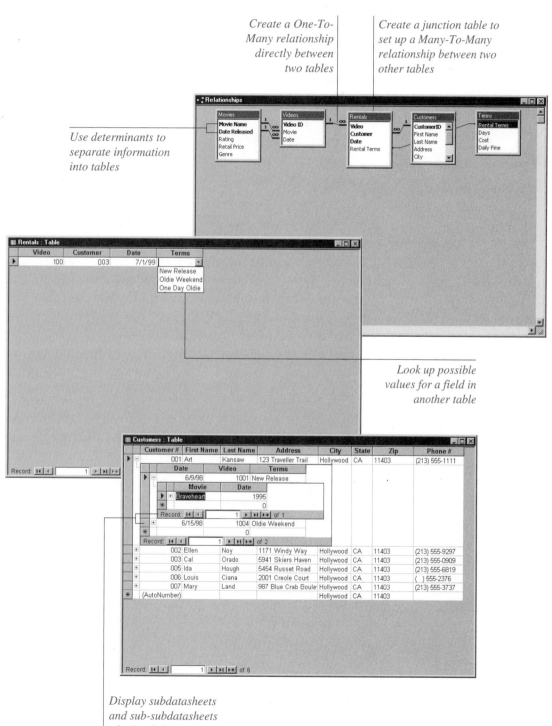

Create a One-To-Many relationship directly between two tables

Create a junction table to set up a Many-To-Many relationship between two other tables

Use determinants to separate information into tables

Look up possible values for a field in another table

Display subdatasheets and sub-subdatasheets of related data

Until now, you have created a few stand-alone database components using Access tools, but you haven't yet learned how to create a relational database. Entire Ph.D. theses have been written on the subject, but a few simple rules are all you need to keep most small to midsize relational databases in shape. It's important to realize that although there are many ways to create a database, some ways are more efficient than others. You will need to balance added efficiency with expediency when deciding how much effort to put into designing your databases. The larger the database, the more important good design becomes.

Rules for Database Design

To understand the concepts behind database design and how good design can help you create a more efficient storage tool, let's examine the South Ridge Video database you created in Part One of this book. The video store has customers and movies, and to keep track of them, you have already set up Customers and Movies tables. But you also want to keep track of rental transactions involving both customers and movies. Does that mean it would be best to keep customer and movie information in one big Transactions table?

Let's say for the sake of argument that you decide to create this Transactions table. When Art Kansaw comes in to rent Braveheart, you enter a record containing this information:

Date	Name	Address	Phone	Movie	Price	Type	Rate
7/1/99	Art Kansaw	123 Traveller Trail Hollywood, CA 11403	(213) 555-1111	Braveheart (1995)	$19.99	Drama/R	$3.50

Obviously, such a table is cumbersome for several reasons:

- The table contains so much data that it's hard to isolate individual items of information. For example, finding PG-rated action movies from the '70s would be very difficult.

- Features such as list boxes and drop-down lists, which help speed up data entry, are not available because each field has too many possible entries.

- A lot of information is repeated. Each time Art Kansaw rents a movie, you have to retype his name and address. Each time someone rents Braveheart, you have to retype the movie information. The database will grow rapidly as you store the same information over and over. In the database world, this is called *redundancy*.

                                                                                        ← Redundancy

- If you delete a record, you risk deleting information you want to save. For example, if Art Kansaw moves to Seattle, you can't delete his records without destroying information about the movies he has rented. In the database world, this is called an *update anomaly*.

                                                                                        ← Update anomalies

- If Art changes his phone number, you have to change it in every one of his records. Otherwise, someone might pull up the wrong information and call his old number. This is another example of an update anomaly.

Solving these problems is called *normalization*. We will not deal exhaustively with normalization, but we will give you three basic rules that will help you design your database in a way that avoids these problems.

                                                                                        ← Normalization

Rule 1: Keep Information Compartmentalized

To properly sort and retrieve information, you need to separate individual items of information and put them in different fields. This rule may seem obvious, but you'd be surprised how many people create Name fields like the example on the facing page and then realize later that they can't sort a table on people's last names. The example's Movie field also demonstrates the need for this rule. You might argue that using this field to find movies by the date of release would be easy using wildcards (see page 64), but the table would quickly become difficult to manage and could be corrupted by entries such as 1984 (1984) and 1941 (1979). So Rule 1 of database design requires that you separate the Name field into First Name and Last Name fields as you did in the Customers table of the South Ridge Video database, and that you separate the Movie field into Movie Name and Date Released fields as you did in the Movies table.

An exception to Rule 1

An exception to Rule 1 of database design is the date, which contains day, month, and year data and may seem cumbersome at first. However, using input masks, default values, and drop-down lists makes entering dates easy, and it is much easier to retrieve entire dates than to retrieve their component parts.

Rule 2: Separate Information Using Determinants

If you just worked with Rule 1, you could still create one big table containing all the information, and you would still have redundancy. The solution to this problem is to create separate, related tables. But how do you decide what information to spin off into a separate table?

Tables generally are designed around a kind of theme, such as movies, customers, or employees. In many cases, using your intuition about what should be in one table and what should be in another works just fine. But when intuition fails, you can fall back on Rule 2 of database design. The trick is to find one or more fields that determine the other fields. Database designers call this field or fields the *determinant.* The determinant then becomes the primary key for the table.

Determinants

To find out if one field (X) is a determinant of another field (Y), ask this question: "If you know the value in field X, do you know the value in field Y?" For example, in a list of employees, you ask: "If you know the Social Security Number field value, do you know the First Name and Last Name field values?" The answer is "Yes" because every social security number is unique. Now let's look at a question from the South Ridge Video database: "If you know the Movie Name field value, do you know the Date Released, Rating, Price, and Genre field values?" If you think about it, the answer is "No" because you have two movies called Frankenstein. But suppose you modify the question to "If you know the Movie Name and Date Released field values, do you then know the Rating, Price, and Genre field values?" Then the answer would most likely be "Yes." So you can say that Movie Name and Date Released determine Rating, Price, and Genre.

Let's apply Rule 2 of database design to the Movies table of the South Ridge Video database, by deleting the ID field and designating the Movie Name and Date Released fields as the table's primary key:

1. Start Access and open the South Ridge Video database. Open the Movies table in design view by selecting Movies and

Flat vs. relational databases

A flat database consists of a single, often very large, table from which you can extract individual items of information. But you can work only with the information in that one table. A relational database can have many tables; and fields in one table can be related to fields in other tables, enabling you to work with the information in all the tables.

clicking the Design button or by right-clicking Movies and choosing Design from the shortcut menu.

2. Point to the primary-key symbol in the ID field selector, and when the pointer changes to a right arrow, click to select the entire field. Then press Delete.

Deleting fields

3. When Access asks whether you want to permanently delete the field, click Yes. Click Yes again when Access warns you that the field is a primary key.

4. Now drag through the selectors for the Movie Name and Date Released fields.

5. Click the Primary Key button on the toolbar. Here are the results:

The Primary Key button

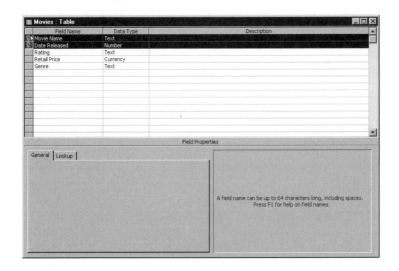

With these two fields as the primary key, Access won't allow two movies with the same name and release date in this table.

Now let's turn our attention to the Customers table. If you know a customer's first and last names, do you know the address? The answer is "Yes" for the customers you've entered so far. But what if you have two customers called John Smith? To account for this possibility, you would have to add a third field to come up with a determinant. In some cases, you know that a set of information (in this case, about customers) should be in one table but the determinant is too complicated. If this happens, it's best to let Access set the primary key by creating an AutoNumber field, or you can create a unique customer ID yourself. (Why do you suppose every merchant you deal with gives you a new account number?)

Rule 3: Move Partial Dependencies to a Linked Table

Suppose South Ridge Video has 20 copies of Braveheart. How should you keep records for them? How do you know which copies have been rented and how many you have left? Your intuition may be to turn the Movies table into a Videos table that includes a Video ID field, like this:

But there are several problems with this new Videos table:

- You would have to enter the Braveheart information 20 times instead of once.

- If the store acquired copies of the movie at different times, different employees might enter the Genre field value as Action, or even Horror, instead of Drama. Inadvertent errors like this one could mean quite a bit of repair work later.

Partially dependent fields → • This table has *partially dependent* fields. These are fields that are dependent on some of the other fields in the table, but not all of them. Here, Rating, Price, and Genre are determined by Movie Name and Date Released, but not by Video ID.

You can solve this type of problem by following Rule 3 of database design, which requires that you keep partially dependent fields in a table of their own and that you link their table to any related table using a *foreign key*. The foreign key then allows you to look up information in the related table instead of repeating it. This rule may require some trade-offs in efficiency vs. expediency. For example, you could create a comprehensive table of zip codes and their corresponding cities and states. Then whenever a table contained address information, as the Customers table does, you could use a foreign key for the Zip code field, omit the City and State fields, and have Access look up the city and state when necessary. But for most databases, you would probably leave the partially dependent City and State fields and accept a little inefficiency rather than spend time creating the zip-code table.

Foreign keys

Efficiency vs. expediency

To apply Rule 3 to the Videos table shown on the facing page, you need to think about movies and the way they are used in the video store. In reality, only one movie called Braveheart was released in 1995, but the store has several copies of it. You have movies, and you have copies of movies called videos. So what you need is one table for movies—the Movies table you have already created—and a separate table for videos—a new table that identifies all the copies of each movie. Isn't that redundant? No. Let's create the Videos table and see why:

1. The Movies table is still open in design view and the Movie Name and Date Released fields are selected. Click the Copy button on the toolbar and close the Movies table, saving your changes.

Copying fields

2. In the Tables list in the Database window, double-click Create Table In Design View.

3. Name the first field *Video ID* and assign the Number data type. Click the Primary Key button on the toolbar.

4. Next click the selector for the second field to highlight the entire field, and then click the Paste button on the toolbar. Access pastes in the definitions for the Movie Name and Date Released fields from the Movies table.

5. Now change the names of the second and third fields to *Movie* and *Date*.

6. Close the table, saving it as *Videos*.

You have now isolated the partially dependent fields. However, Access does not yet know that the Movie and Date fields in Videos are related to the Movie Name and Date Released fields in Movies. The copy-and-paste operation has transferred only the definitions of the fields. You need to establish a relationship between the two tables to let Access know that the data in these fields should correspond. Then if you need additional information about a video, such as its rating, Access can look in the Movies table to find it.

Establishing Relationships

You create relationships between tables so that you can combine the information from more than one table in queries, forms, data access pages, and reports. A relationship is formed by matching the primary-key field in one table with the foreign-key field in another table. As you already know, the values in a primary-key field must be unique. The values in a foreign-key field need not be unique, but each one should match a value in the corresponding primary-key field. Access provides a method called *referential integrity* to ensure the field values match.

Referential integrity ⟶

You can create these three types of relationships between two tables:

Types of relationships ⟶

- **One-To-Many.** A record that is unique in one table can have many corresponding records in the other table. For example, the value Braveheart occurs only once in the Movie Name field of the Movies table, but it can occur many times in the Movie field of the Videos table.

- **One-To-One.** A record that is unique in one table is also unique in the other table. This type of relationship is rare.

- **Many-To-Many.** A record that is unique in one table can have many corresponding records in the other table and vice versa. For example, each customer in the Customers table can rent many videos in the Videos table, and each video in the Videos table can be rented by many customers.

Don't worry if this sounds confusing. In this section, you'll create a couple of One-To-Many relationships and a Many-To-Many relationship so that you can see how they work.

Creating a One-To-Many Relationship

Let's start by forging a relationship between the Movies and Videos tables so that Access will know that the data in the Movie Name and Date Released fields in Movies correspond with the data in the Movie and Date fields in Videos:

1. Click the Relationships button on the toolbar. Access opens the Relationships window and displays this dialog box:

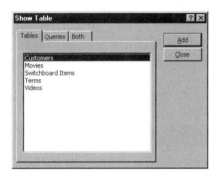

The Relationships button

2. Double-click first Movies and then Videos to add these tables to the Relationships window, and then close the Show Table dialog box. The Relationships window looks like this:

Defining the relationship

3. In the Movies box, select the Movie Name field, hold down the Shift key, and select the Date Released field.

4. Point to the selection, hold down the left mouse button, and drag to the Videos box. When you release the mouse button, the dialog box shown below appears:

5. Click the first edit box under Videos in the Related Table/Query column, click the arrow button, and select Movie from the drop-down list.

6. Click the second edit box and select Date.

7. Next click the Enforce Referential Integrity check box to turn on referential integrity. This step is essential if you want to reduce update anomalies and redundancy (see page 89). When this box is checked, Access won't allow you to enter Movie and Date values in the Videos table unless corresponding Movie Name and Date Released values exist in the Movies table. For example, if you try to enter *Brveheart* in the Movie field of the Videos table, Access will display an error message.

8. The Relationship Type at the bottom of the dialog box is set to One-To-Many to tell Access that each movie is listed once in the Movies table but can show up many times in the Videos table. Click Create. Access closes the dialog box and indicates the new relationship, as shown here:

Join types

You will rarely use the Join Type button in the Edit Relationships dialog box, but you may want to know what it does. You click this button when you want to tell Access how to use this relationship in queries. When Access runs a query using this relationship, the first option tells it to show only the records where fields from both tables match. The second option tells Access to show all the records in the first table and the matching records in the second table. The third option tells Access to show all the records in the second table and the matching records in the first table.

9. Close the Relationships window, clicking Yes to save the new relationship when prompted.

Now let's test the relationship by giving South Ridge Video store some inventory. Follow these steps to add records to the Videos table:

1. Open the Videos table and enter the following information:

Testing referential integrity

Video ID	Movie	Date
1000	Braveheart	1995
1001	Braveheart	1995
1002	Braveheart	1995
1003	Casablanca	1942
1004	Cinderella	1950
1005	Frankenstein	1993
1006	Titanic	1997

When you try to move to the next record after entering Titanic, Access displays this error message:

Microsoft Access

You cannot add or change a record because a related record is required in table 'Movies'.

OK   Help

2. Click OK to close the message box, and then click the Undo button on the toolbar to clear the Titanic record.

The Undo button

3. Close the Videos table.

Creating a Many-To-Many Relationship

Now that you have a feel for relationships, you are ready to create the main relationship of the South Ridge Video database: between the Customers and Videos tables. This relationship is Many-To-Many because each customer can rent many videos and each video can be rented by many customers. You can't create a Many-To-Many relationship directly. Instead you must create a new table, called a *junction table*, that includes fields with the same definitions as the primary-key fields from the two tables. You then establish One-To-Many relationships between each of the two tables and the junction table.

Junction tables

To create a Many-To-Many relationship between the Customers and Videos tables, you'll set up a junction table called *Rentals*. Follow these steps:

1. Click the arrow to the right of the New Object button on the toolbar and select Table from the drop-down list.

2. In the New Table dialog box, select Design View and click OK.

3. Define the following fields:

Field	Data Type	Field Properties
Video	Number	
Customer	Number	Format = 000
Date	Date/Time	Format = Short Date

4. Select the Video, Customer, and Date fields and click the Primary Key button on the toolbar.

Why do you need all three fields as the primary key? If you know the Video and Customer values, do you know the Date value? No, a customer might rent the same video on different days. If you know the Customer and Date values, do you know the Video value? Only if you restrict customers to one video a day. Do the Date and Video values tell you the Customer value? It's possible, but if someone rents a video in the morning and returns it in the afternoon, you can't rent the video again that day without corrupting the database. So you need all three fields to identify a unique rental transaction.

5. Close the Table window, saving the table as *Rentals*.

Having created the junction table, let's now create relationships with the Customers and Videos tables:

1. Click the Relationships button to display the Relationships window.

The Show Table button

2. Click the Show Table button, and in the Show Table dialog box, double-click Customers and Rentals to add them to the Relationships window, and then close the Show Table dialog box. The Relationships window now looks like the one shown at the top of the facing page.

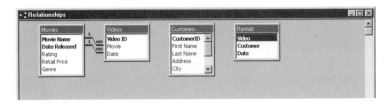

3. Rearrange the boxes so that the Rentals box sits between the Videos and Customers boxes. (Drag the boxes by their title bars to move them.)

4. Now click the Video ID field in the Videos box and drag it over the Video field in the Rentals box. Access displays the Edit Relationships dialog box (shown earlier on page 102), where Video is already assigned under Rentals in the Related Table/Query column.

5. Click the Enforce Referential Integrity check box and then click Create.

6. Repeat steps 4 and 5 to create a One-To-Many relationship by dragging Customer ID in the Customers box over Customer in the Rentals box. Access indicates the two new relationships as shown below:

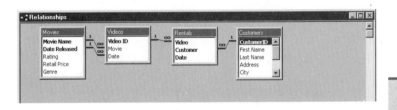

7. Close the Relationships window, saving your changes.

Creating a Relationship Using the Lookup Wizard

To make the Rentals table even more useful, let's include a field to hold the terms of each rental transaction. You may recall that the South Ridge Video database already includes a Terms table that spells out what terms are available. To ensure that only valid term data is used in the Rentals table, you can create a relationship between a Terms field in the Rentals

Changing or deleting relationships

Editing or deleting relationships is easy in Access. In the Relationships window, right-click the lighter middle part of the line indicating the relationship you want to change or delete. Then choose Edit Relationship or Delete from the shortcut menu that appears. If you choose Edit Relationship, Access displays the Edit Relationships dialog box (shown on page 102) so you can make changes.

table and the Rental Terms field of the Terms table. This time, you'll create the relationship using the Lookup Wizard. Follow these steps:

1. Open the Rentals table in design view and add a new field below Date called *Terms*.

2. In the Data Type column, click the arrow button and select Lookup Wizard from the drop-down list. The wizard displays its first dialog box (shown earlier on page 42).

3. With the Look Up The Values option selected, click Next to display the dialog box shown here:

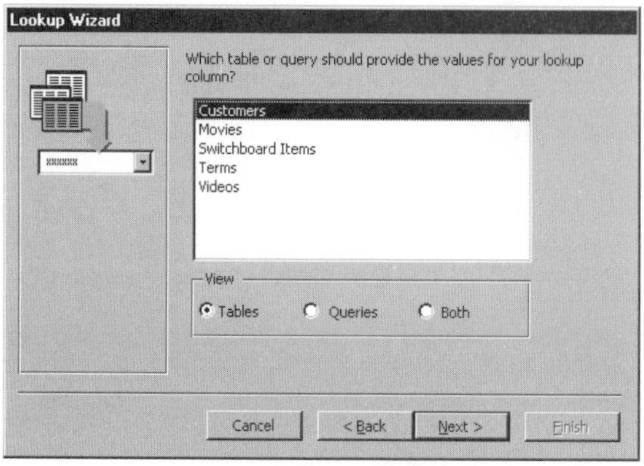

4. Double-click Terms to both select it and move to this dialog box:

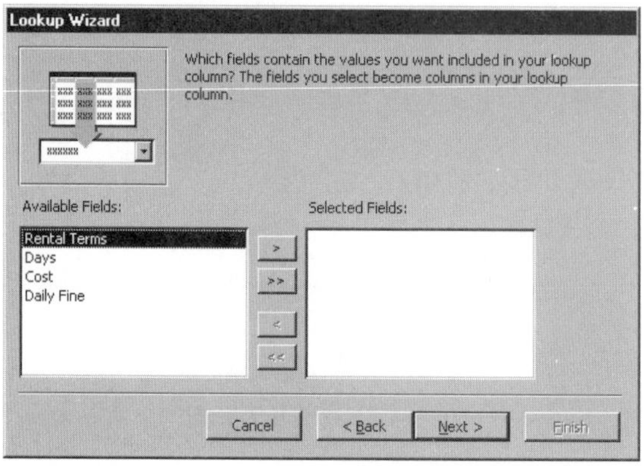

5. With Rental Terms selected, click the > button and then click Next to display the dialog box shown on the facing page.

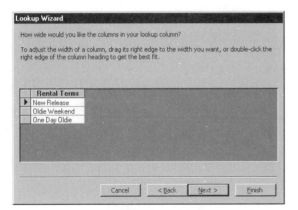

6. Click Finish and then click Yes to save the table and the new relationship. The Table window now looks like this:

Notice that Access has changed the name of the new field to correspond with that of the Rental Terms field in the Terms table. The name you typed in step 1, Terms, is now the new field's caption.

7. With the Rental Terms field active, click the Lookup tab in the Field Properties section, and change the Limit To List property to Yes.

To take a look at the results of this procedure, follow the steps on the next page.

1. Switch to datasheet view, saving your changes to the table. Then click the Terms field in the first record and click the arrow button. A drop-down list appears with the Rental Terms from the Terms table, like this:

Cascading updates and deletions

Two additional options become available in the Edit Relationships dialog box after you click the Enforce Referential Integrity check box. Click the Cascade Update Related Fields check box to tell Access to update corresponding values in a related table when changes are made to the primary-key value in the primary table. (If the primary-key field in your table is set to AutoNumber, clicking this option will have no effect since you can't change values in AutoNumber fields.) Click the Cascade Delete Related Records check box to tell Access that when you delete a record in the primary table, Access should delete any corresponding records in the related table. By turning on these options, you override the default settings, which prevent updating and deleting when the Enforce Referential Integrity option is checked.

2. Close the Table window, click the Relationships button to open the Relationships window, and enlarge the Rentals box so that you can see the new Rental Terms field. (Drag its bottom border downward.)

3. Click the Show Table button, and in the Show Table dialog box, double-click Terms to add it to the Relationships window. Then click Close. The results are shown here:

As you can see, the Lookup Wizard has created a relationship between the Terms and Rentals tables.

4. Close the Relationships window, saving your changes.

Let's take some time now to fine-tune the Rentals table and enter a few rental transactions:

1. Open the Rentals table in design view, where the fields are listed in the order in which you created them.

2. Rental transactions would logically be entered in date order, so click the selector for the Date field, point to the selector, and drag the selected field to the top of the field list. Then move the Customer field above the Video field.

3. Switch back to datasheet view, saving your changes.

4. Type *6/1/99* in the Date field, *1* in the Customer field, *1001* in the Video field, and *New* in the Terms field. As soon as you type the *N*, Access finds a match in the Rental Terms field of the Terms table and highlights it in the Terms field. You can then press Enter to move to the next record. This data entry shortcut is made possible by a feature called AutoCorrect. (See the adjacent tip for more information.)

5. Now enter these records:

Date	Customer	Video	Terms
6/5/99	1	1004	Oldie Weekend
6/8/99	2	1005	One Day Oldie
6/11/99	5	1000	New Release
6/12/99	3	1004	Oldie Weekend

6. Widen the Terms column so that you can see all the entries and then close the Rentals table, saving your changes.

Viewing Related Data

Access reflects existing table relationships in a way that allows you to see the linked information with a single mouse-click. Follow these steps to check this out:

1. Open the Customers table, and notice the new column on the left that contains plus signs, as shown on the next page.

More about AutoCorrect

Some users appreciate Auto-Correct's assistance and others don't. AutoCorrect is turned on by default. To turn it off, choose AutoCorrect from the expanded Tools menu and then deselect the Replace Text As You Type option. Other options at the top of the dialog box take care of common typing "errors." Access can correct two initial capital letters in a word, correct sentences that don't begin with a capital letter, capitalize the days of the week, and correct accidental usage of the Caps Lock Key. You can turn any of these options on or off by clicking the corresponding check box. If you click the Exceptions button, you can tell Access not to capitalize the word immediately following an abbreviated word (such as *apt.* for *apartment*). Or you can tell Access not to correct two consecutive initial capital letters in certain instances. If you find this feature useful, you can also use the AutoCorrect dialog box to assign your own shorthand words. For example, you might type *ws* in the Replace edit box, type *widescreen format* in the With edit box, and click Add. Then you can type *ws* in a field, and Access will insert *widescreen format* when you move to the next field. If you scan the list in the AutoCorrect dialog box, you will notice that AutoCorrect will also automatically fix several common spelling errors.

The plus signs indicate the availability of data at a lower hierarchical level, like the plus signs in Windows Explorer.

Displaying subdatasheets

2. Click the plus sign for Art Kansaw, customer number 001, to see this *subdatasheet* of information from the Rentals table:

Parent and child tables

The Customers table, as you recall, has a one-to-many relationship to the Rentals table; in other words, the Customers information is held in the *parent table* and the Rentals information is held in the *child table*. The subdatasheet above contains only the child information for Art Kansaw.

Now let's test the link between the Customers and Rentals tables by making a change in the subdatasheet:

1. Replace the date of the first rental, *6/1/99*, with *6/9/99* and click the second record to complete the change.

The Database Window button

2. Click the Database Window button on the toolbar to display the Database window. Your screen looks like the one shown on the facing page.

3. Open the Rentals table to verify that customer number 001 rented video number 1001 on 6/9/99.

You want to know which movies Art Kansaw rented, but you don't know their video IDs by heart. Because you established a many-to-many relationship between the Customers and Videos tables (via the Rentals junction table), you can tailor the Customers table to show a sub-subdatasheet. Try this:

1. Close the Rentals table and then click the Customers table to activate it.

2. Select the Video column in the subdatasheet and choose Sub-datasheet from the Insert menu to open this dialog box:

Displaying sub-subdatasheets

3. Select Videos in the Tables list, select Video ID from the Link Child Fields drop-down list, and then select video from the Link Master Fields list. Then click OK.

4. If Access displays a dialog box saying that it doesn't detect a relationship between the Video ID and Video fields, click Yes to create the relationship.

5. Now click the plus sign for the 6/9/99 rental to see the subdatasheet shown here:

As you can see, Art Kansaw rented Braveheart on 6/9/99. Notice the plus sign next to Braveheart. If you click that plus sign, Access displays the Insert Subdatasheet dialog box so that you can select another set of child information. Refrain from clicking plus signs after you have the information you seek.

6. Close the Customers table, saving your changes to the Rentals table when prompted.

Now let's test the many-to-many relationship from the other direction. Follow these steps:

1. Open the Videos table and expand the subdatasheet of rental information for video number 1001. (If Access displays the Insert Subdatasheet dialog box, select the Rentals table, check that the Link Child Fields option is Video and the Link Master Fields option is Video ID, and click OK. Then click Yes if prompted to create the relationship.)

2. Next expand the 6/9/99 record in the Rentals subdatasheet, as shown on the facing page.

Removing subdatasheets

To remove a default subdatasheet from a table, open the table in design view and click the Properties button. In the Properties dialog box, click the Subdatasheet Name edit box, click its arrow, and select [None] from the drop-down list. If you manually add a subdatasheet to a table and later change your mind, set the Subdatasheet Name property to [None] and save the changes. Then you can reset the Subdatasheet Name property to [Auto].

3. Close the Videos table. (If prompted, save your changes.)

Because you've already set the Rentals junction table to show movie names for video IDs, the third level subdatasheet repeats the data in the first level datasheet. You could alter the subdatasheets to show customer information at the third level, but you are more likely to want the Customers table to expand to show rentals and movie names than for the Videos table to show rentals and customers. Besides, there are more efficient ways than subdatasheets to extract information from multiple tables, which we discuss in Chapter 5. For now, let's explore some of the tools Access provides for reducing errors.

Design Techniques for Reducing Errors

You have already learned about several tools that help keep errors to a minimum, including primary keys, default values, input masks, combo/list boxes, and referential integrity. In this section, you will explore a few more tools that help you and the people who use your databases avoid mistakes.

Using Formulas as Default Values

In Chapter 2, we discussed using default values in the City, State, and PostalCode fields to save input effort and help avoid errors. You can also set a default value based on a formula to be calculated by Access. For example, in the Rentals table of the South Ridge Video database, you will rarely enter a date that is not the current date. People don't rent videos yesterday or tomorrow; they rent them today. So why not have Access enter the current date each time you make an entry? Follow these steps:

1. Open the Rentals table in design view, click anywhere in the Date field, and click the Default Value edit box in the Field Properties section.

The Build button

2. Click the Build button on the toolbar or click the Build button to the right of the edit box to display this dialog box:

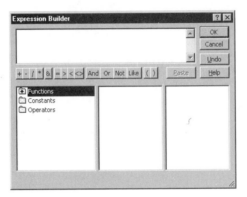

The Expression Builder

The *Expression Builder* is a very useful tool for manipulating data in Access. For example, you can use it to create formulas (equations) based on the values in other fields or on functions built into Access. The possibilities are virtually limitless. For now, you are going to use a simple function called *Date()*, which pulls the date from your computer's built-in clock/calendar and inserts it in the selected field.

Using built-in functions

3. Double-click the Functions folder and then click the Built-In Functions subfolder. Access displays categories of functions in the second list box and lists the functions in the selected category in the third list box.

4. Click Date/Time in the second box and double-click Date in the third box. The dialog box now looks like the one shown at the top of the facing page.

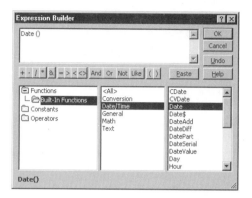

5. Click OK. Then close the table, saving your changes.

Now whenever a record is added to the Rentals table, the current date will appear by default in the Date field.

Be careful to use formulas only when they are necessary. For example, you might be tempted to add a new field to the Rentals table called Date Due and to build a formula such as Date() + 1 as the field's default value. However, if you know the date the video was rented and the terms, you know the date due. There is no need to keep track of it because you can easily derive the date due from two pieces of information you already have. If you create a new field to store this information, you introduce redundancy, and after a few thousand rentals, your database will be bigger and slower than it needs to be.

Validation Rules

In Chapter 2's discussion of field properties, we skipped over the Validation Rule and Validation Text properties because it makes more sense to discuss them in the context of database design. When you set a validation rule for a field, Access allows only field values that meet the rule to be entered in the field. The kind of rule you can set up varies with the field's data type. You can specify that a text field should contain one of a set of values—for example, the City field should contain only Hollywood or Beverly. You can specify that a date field should contain only the current date or a date that falls within a certain range. With number fields, you can specify that Access should accept only a specific value or a value that

Other date/time functions

In addition to the Date() function, you can use other functions to work with date/time information. The two most common functions are Time(), which returns the time of day, and Now(), which returns the current date and time. If you want to explore other date/time functions, you can enter the name of the function on the Index tab of the Help window. For example, entering *DatePart*, then clicking Search, and double-clicking a topic gives you more information about that function.

falls within a range. You can also specify that the values in a field must match the values in the same field in another table.

Let's look at an example. In the Movies table, the Date Released field has the Number data type. (You could have used the Date/Time data type, but you are interested only in the year, so why complicate things?) An employee could enter *1895* instead of *1985* in this field, and Access would accept it. To avoid this kind of data input error, you want the values in this field to fall between 1900 and, say, 2050. Follow these steps to create the necessary rule:

1. Open the Movies table in design view and click anywhere in the Date Released field.

Building a validation formula

2. Click the Validation Rule edit box in the Field Properties section, and then click the Build button to the right of the edit box to display the Expression Builder dialog box.

3. Click the > button, type *1900*, click the And button, click the < button, and type *2050*. Then if necessary, delete *Expr* and its enclosing chevrons, which Access may have inserted before the < symbol. The Expression Builder dialog box looks like this:

4. Click OK to close the dialog box and enter the formula in the Validation Rule edit box.

Adding validation text

5. Click the Validation Text edit box, and type *Value must be between 1900 and 2050*. Access will display this message whenever an unacceptable value is entered.

6. Switch to datasheet view, save the changes to the table's structure, and click Yes when Access asks whether you want it to test existing data in the Date Released field against the new validation rule.

Now for the acid test:

1. Change the Date Released field value for Cinderella to *11*, and then try moving to another record. Access displays the message box shown here:

2. Click OK in the message box and press the Esc key to restore the original value in the Date Released field.

3. Close the Table window.

As you can see, validation rules are powerful tools that can help you ensure the accuracy of your data. The need for a validation rule may not be apparent when you first create a table; you may identify the need only after problems begin to show up. So it's good to know that you can always go back and add these safeguards later.

Protecting Your Data

If you are running Access on your own computer at work or at home, you probably don't have to worry about the kinds of conflicts that can arise when more than one person has access to the same database. However, if you share a computer, you might have concerns about protecting your data, and if you work on a network, protecting your data becomes a necessity. You can lock a record or an entire database to temporarily control access, and you can create passwords to control access more permanently. We talk about security and passwords in Chapter 6. Here we'll take a quick look at the temporary protection methods.

Backing up

Regularly backing up your files is an important aspect of database security. In addition to copying your database files to disks or tape for storage away from your computer, you might want to create a Backup folder in which you can store a copy of your working files to protect against inadvertent changes.

Unlike many applications that wait for you to tell them when to save information, Access saves the values in a new or edited record as soon as you move to another record. As a result, two or more people on a network can work on the same table at the same time. To prevent someone else from working on the record you are working on, you can lock the record. Follow these steps:

Locking records

1. Choose Options from the Tools menu to display the Options dialog box, and then click the Advanced tab to display the options shown below:

Notice the three options in the Default Record Locking section. No Locks is the default. The Edited Record option locks the record that is being edited in a table, form, or query and is appropriate for when you only occasionally have two or more people working on the same database at the same time. The All Records option not only locks all of the records in an open table, form, or query, it also locks all related tables. All Records is the most conservative option, because it can have the effect of locking the entire database file until you close it. It is the best option if several people often work on the same database and data integrity is a very high priority.

(For more information about the options on this tab, click the ? button in the top right corner of the dialog box and then click the options you are curious about to display a pop-up description box.)

2. You won't apply any locks at this time, so click Cancel to close the Options dialog box.

You've learned a good deal about database design in this chapter, and some of the concepts may seem confusing. If it's any consolation, few people can set up a database correctly right off the bat. You should always play around with dummy data to start with, so that you can go back and change things until you get them right. It can be frustrating, it can be a challenge, and once in a while, it's even fun!

5

More Sophisticated Forms and Queries

You create multi-table forms and then add subforms, command buttons, and field formulas. We then demonstrate ways you can use forms and queries together to increase data-input efficiency and better display extracted data.

Using forms and queries together can be an invaluable way of getting information out of any database, especially if you want to track items such as library books, student papers, or bank accounts.

Forms and queries created and concepts covered:

Use unbound controls in a form to perform calculations

Enter data in two tables at once by using subforms

Create a graph based on a table or query

In Part One, you created forms and queries that worked with the data in single tables and used very simple functions. In this chapter, you'll see how forms and queries can work with several tables and can include complex functions that make a database easier to use. As you learned in Chapter 4, good database design tends to increase the number of tables in a database, which in turn increases the number of relationships and primary and foreign keys that you have to deal with. To avoid confusion, you can use forms and queries to create an intuitive interface that requires no knowledge of the underlying structure of the database. You'll look at both forms and queries in this chapter, starting with forms.

Creating Multi-Table Forms

As you know, forms are a useful way of entering or editing data in a single table, but you can also use forms to view, add, or edit data in multiple tables. That's what makes them so powerful. Someone can enter information in just one form, and behind the scenes, Access will shuffle the individual items into their designated tables.

Forms and relationships

When you create a form based on two or more tables, you can take advantage of any existing relationships. Access traces the relationships through as many tables as necessary to find the correct information. As a demonstration, let's create a form for entering new rental transactions in the South Ridge Video database. In addition to showing all the fields in the Rentals table, it will show the customer name (from the Customers table), the movie name (from the Videos table), and the movie rating (from the Movies table). Follow these steps:

1. Start Access and open the South Ridge Video database.

2. Create a new form using the Form Wizard.

Specifying multiple tables

3. Select Table: Rentals from the Tables/Queries drop-down list and move all of its fields to the Selected Fields box. Then select Table: Videos from the drop-down list and move Movie to the Selected Fields box. Select Table: Movies and move

Rating. Finally, select Table: Customers and move First Name and Last Name. Then click Next.

4. In the next few dialog boxes, leave By Rentals as the viewing option and Columnar as the layout option. Leave Standard as the style option and Rentals as the form's title. Click Finish to display the form, which looks like this:

The record for the first video rental appears in the first four fields, followed by the information from the Videos, Movies, and Customers tables.

Did you notice that you have a problem waiting to happen with this form? As things stand, someone could change the First Name field to *Bob*. Because this form is intended to be used to enter rentals, not edit movie information or customer names, you should not only make the Rating, First Name, and Last Name fields unavailable, but also make it clear on the form that the user shouldn't even try to change them. Follow these steps:

1. Switch to design view and maximize the Form window. If necessary, close the Toolbox by clicking its Close button, or dock it.

2. Increase the width of the Detail section's grid, delete some labels, adjust the size of others, and then move the controls so that your form looks like the one shown on the next page. (If you need a refresher on sizing and moving labels and controls, refer to page 74.)

The trouble with wizards

Wizards are powerful tools that help you accomplish many tasks. But if you create objects using wizards and then try to go back and modify them, you might run into error messages you do not understand. Sometimes it's easier to go back and recreate the object rather than modify a wizard-created one.

3. You don't want the Rating value to be changed in this form, and leaving the Rating control as a combo box is too tempting. Right-click the control and choose Change To and then Text Box from the shortcut menu.

Disabling fields

4. With the Rating control still selected, hold down the Shift key and click the First Name, Last Name, and Movie controls to add them to the selection. Then right-click one of the selected controls, choose Properties from the shortcut menu, change the Enabled property on the Data tab to No, and close the Properties dialog box. Access changes the background color of the selected controls and dims the text. (You can't customize either of these control elements, but you can change the border color.)

Setting forms for new data entry only

5. Finally, double-click the form selector at the junction of the horizontal and vertical rulers to display the Properties dialog box for the entire form. Then change the Data Entry property to Yes and close the dialog box.

6. Now save the form.

By changing the form's Data Entry property, you specify that the form should be used only for creating new entries. You cannot scroll back through existing rentals. Let's add some more rentals now to see how the form reacts:

1. Switch to form view, where the new form looks like this:

2. Enter the following rental transactions:

Date	Customer	Video	Rental Terms
6/19/99	5	1004	Oldie Weekend
6/24/99	5	1005	One Day Oldie
6/25/99	2	1002	New Release
6/28/99	3	1001	New Release

3. Close the Rentals form. Notice that because you maximized the Form window, Access assumes you want all windows maximized for the current session.

4. Just to confirm that the form has done its job, open the Rentals table, which is sorted by video ID and contains four new records. Then close it.

Adding Subforms

Sometimes you'll want to enter information in two or more related tables using one form. The best format for achieving this level of efficiency is a main form with one or more subforms. For example, you currently enter a new movie record in the Movies table and then enter the video records for that movie in the Videos table. It may seem like a lot of work to open one form and enter a movie, and then open another form and repeat some of the same information to record each video. Because these two tables are related, you can use a main form with a subform to make the process more efficient. You already created a New Movies form in Chapter 2 (see page 47), so now you need to create another form that you can use as a subform. Follow the steps on the next page.

Multi-table reports and data access pages

Reports and data access pages, like forms, sometimes contain information from more than one table. (They can also be based on multiple queries.) For example, if Mitch Egan wants to see which customers are renting which movies on a monthly basis, the report must contain information from the Customers, Rentals, and Videos tables. You can create the report with the Report Wizard, selecting the desired fields from each table in the first dialog box, as you would with the Form Wizard (see page 122). Then continue with the wizard as usual. You can also use existing reports, one as the main report and the other as the subreport. Open the main report in design view, click the Subform/Subreport button on the Toolbox toolbar, and draw a subreport control in the Detail section. The Subreport Wizard walks you through the process of identifying the source report and the fields you want to include in the subreport. You can then reformat the resulting subreport to suit your needs. Both of these methods can also be used for multi-table data access pages.

1. First use the Form Wizard to create a new form based on the Videos table. Move only the Video ID field to the Selected Fields box and then click Finish to accept the wizard's remaining default settings.

2. Switch to design view, where the form looks like this:

Specifying the default view

3. Double-click the form selector to display the Properties dialog box, change the Default View setting on the Format tab to Datasheet, and close the dialog box.

4. Close the Form window, saving your changes.

   Now you need to tell Access that the Videos form is a subform of the New Movies form. Here's how:

1. Open the New Movies form in design view, and if necessary, close the Movies Field List box.

2. You have deleted the ID field from the Movies table (the basis for this form), so delete both the ID control and its label.

3. Now move and resize the controls and their labels, like this:

Handy helpers

To save time as you work on the design of a form, you can open the Properties dialog box, Toolbox toolbar, and Field List window and leave them open while you switch between form view and design view. All three of these tools stay open when you switch to form view, though the Toolbox toolbar and Field List box are hidden. Then when you switch back to design view, the tools are available if you need them.

4. If necessary, click the Toolbox button on the toolbar to display its toolbar, and then click the Subform/Subreport button.

The Subform/Subreport button

5. Move the subform pointer to the right of the Movie Name control and click once to create a frame in the Details grid. Access displays the Subform Wizard's first dialog box, shown below. (You may have to install the wizard first.)

The Subform Wizard

SubForm Wizard

You can use an existing form to create your subform or subreport, or create your own using tables and/or queries.

What data would you like to use for your subform or subreport?

○ Use existing Tables and Queries
○ Use an existing form

New Customers
Rentals
Switchboard
Videos

| Cancel | < Back | Next > | Finish |

6. Click the Use An Existing Form option, select Videos from the list below, and click Next to display this dialog box:

SubForm Wizard

Would you like to define which fields link your main form to this subform yourself, or choose from the list below?

○ Choose from a list.   ○ Define my own.

Show Videos for each record in Movies using Movie Name, Date Rele
None

| Cancel | < Back | Next > | Finish |

7. Access has identified the relationship between the two tables and knows how to link them, so click Finish.

8. Back in design view, notice the label lurking behind the new subform. Click the arrow to the right of the Object box at the left end of the Formatting toolbar, scroll the list of form

The Object box

The Object box, located to the left of the Font box on the Formatting toolbar, is a handy feature for working with reports or forms whose objects are not all in view. You can click the box's arrow and select any object on the current form or report from the drop-down list. The object is then highlighted on the form or report, and its name is displayed in the Object box.

elements, and select Videos Label to select the label above and behind the Videos subform control. Then press the Delete key to delete the label.

Sizing subforms

9. Select the subform control and drag its bottom center handle down to enlarge the control so that it aligns with the Rating control.

10. Then double-click the subform's form selector, change the Data Entry property in the Properties dialog box to Yes so that you can enter new videos but not edit existing ones, and close the dialog box.

11. Switch to form view, where the New Movies form now looks like this:

And there you have it! Suppose a new shipment of videos arrives at South Ridge Video—say five copies of Titanic. Let's see the form in action:

Testing the form

1. Tab through the form to see how smoothly the information can be entered into both the New Movies form and the Videos subform.

2. Enter the following information:

Movie Name	Date Released	Genre	Retail Price	Rating
Titanic	1997	Drama	19.99	PG

(Titanic is actually rated PG-13, but if you haven't added a PG-13 rating, you can select PG for now.)

3. Now enter five Video ID values from 1006 to 1010.

4. Close the New Movies form, saving the changes.

5. Open the Movies and Videos tables to verify that the data you entered in the form has been transferred to the tables.

Verifying data entry

By now, you are probably beginning to see how good database design and well-thought-out forms can make data entry easy and efficient.

Adding Command Buttons

One of the most useful tools you can add to a form is a command button. Command buttons allow you to switch to a different form, search for specific records, exit the database, and do a whole host of other tasks. As an example, you'll create a Find button on the New Customers form, so that when you need to change a customer's address or phone number, you can easily search for the correct record. Here are the steps:

1. Open the New Customers form in design view and widen the Detail area. Then click the Command Button button on the Toolbox toolbar.

The Command Button button

2. Move the pointer to the right of the First Name control and click to create a small frame. Access starts the Command Button Wizard and displays its first dialog box:

The Command Button Wizard

Command Button Wizard

Sample:
🔍→

What action do you want to happen when the button is pressed?

Different actions are available for each category.

Categories:
Record Navigation
Record Operations
Form Operations
Report Operations
Application
Miscellaneous

Actions:
Find Next
Find Record
Go to First Record
Go to Last Record
Go to Next Record
Go to Previous Record

Cancel   < Back   Next >   Finish

3. With Record Navigation selected in the Categories list on the left, select Find Record in the Actions list on the right and click Next to display the second dialog box, shown on the next page.

Other command button actions

In the Command Button Wizard's first dialog box, be sure to check in the Categories list to get an idea of the range of actions for which you can create command buttons. Most of the actions are self-explanatory, because they are basic functions of the program.

4. With the Picture option and Binoculars 2 selected, click Next to display this dialog box:

5. In this last dialog box, type *Find Customer* as the name of the button, and click Finish. Here's the result (we've moved the Toolbox out of the way):

Notice that Access has automatically resized the button to fit the graphic you chose in step 4. Because the button is still selected, its name (Find Customer) appears in the Object box at the left end of the Formatting toolbar.

6. Click the Save button to save your changes to the form.

Now let's test the new button:

1. Click the View button on the toolbar to switch to form view, and then click the form's new Find Customer button. Access displays this Find And Replace dialog box:

2. In the Find What edit box, type *5* and click Find Next. Access displays the record for Ida Hough, whose Customer # field value is 005. You can now edit the record if necessary.

3. Click the Cancel button to close the dialog box and then close the Form window.

The ability to create buttons to perform routine actions really enhances what you can do with forms. (If you are interested in programming, you can also create actions with Visual Basic and launch them by clicking command buttons. This topic is beyond the scope of this book, but to find out more you can check the Visual Basic topics in Access's Help feature.)

Visual Basic

Adding the Date

With controls, you can display all sorts of information in a form—some from tables or queries and some from other sources. For example, you can display the current date in the New Movies form by following these steps:

1. Open the New Movies form in design view and decrease the width of the Videos subform control to about ⅞ inch.

ControlTips

By now you are probably familiar with the ScreenTips feature of most Windows applications. You can create similar tips within your database to help the user. Simply type whatever information you want displayed in the ControlTip Text edit box on the Other tab of the Properties dialog box. In form view, this text will appear when the pointer pauses over the control.

2. Click the Text Box button on the Toolbox toolbar, and click the Detail section to the right of the Videos subform control to create a new text-box control. The new control is designated as Unbound because it is not linked to any table, and it has a label identifying it as a text control. (If the label is hidden behind the Videos control, move the new control to the right until you can see it.)

3. Click an insertion point in the new control (the word *Unbound* disappears), type =*Date( )*, and press Enter.

4. Point to the control's border and double-click to display its Properties dialog box. Set the Format property to Short Date and close the dialog box.

5. Select the text in the text box's label, type *Today's Date:*, and press Enter. Then adjust the label's size and reposition the form's elements as necessary to make everything fit.

6. Click the View button on the toolbar to see these results:

7. Close the form, saving your changes.

Adding the time and page number

You could also create controls to show the time (=*Time()*) and page number (=*Page()*).

Using Queries and Forms Together

Using queries and forms together provides a greater degree of flexibility than working with just one or the other. In this section, we'll show you several ways in which you can combine queries and forms to accomplish specific tasks. Bear in mind that our examples can easily be adapted and extended to meet the needs of your own databases.

Using Parameter Queries with Forms

Parameter queries take the work out of locating specific records. Of course, you could open the appropriate table and use the Find command or a filter to do your searching, but these tools take several steps and can be confusing to uninitiated users. Once you have set up a parameter query, simply opening the query displays a dialog box where you enter the record you are looking for. Access then displays that record in a datasheet. As you'll see, you can also combine a parameter query and a form to display the record in a form instead.

Let's say you want to create a form for one of the most basic tasks in the video store: logging in returned videos. For this form all you really need are a Video ID field and a new field to record that the video has been returned. Follow these steps to create a new field called *Returned?* in the Rentals table:

1. Open the Rentals table in design view, add a field called *Returned?*, set its data type to Yes/No, and switch to datasheet view, saving your changes. Notice that Access has put empty check boxes in the Returned? field. An unchecked box represents a No field value, and a checked box represents a Yes field value.

   ← The Yes/No data type

2. In the table, click the Returned? check box for all but the latest transaction for each video. (Obviously, a video must be returned before it can be rented again.)

   With this preparation out of the way, you can set up a parameter query for returned videos. Follow these steps:

1. Click the arrow to the right of the New Object button on the toolbar and select Query from the drop-down list. With Design View selected in the New Query dialog box, click OK.

2. The Rentals box should be displayed in the Query window. If it's not, double-click Rentals in the Show Table dialog box, and then click Close.

What is a parameter?

Programmers and mathematicians know what a parameter is, but the word may be unfamiliar to many users. Think of a parameter as being similar to the criteria you enter in the Criteria row of the QBE grid. It is a piece of information that Access needs in order to be able to carry out a specific task. In our sample parameter query, the parameter you enter identifies the record you are looking for.

3. Double-click the Video and the Returned? fields to add them to the QBE grid.

4. In the Criteria row of the Video column, type *[Enter the video ID number]*. Enclosing the instruction in square brackets tells Access to display the instruction in a dialog box so that you can specify the video you are looking for.

5. In the Criteria row of the Returned? column, type *No*. The Query window now looks like the one shown below. (We widened the first column to display all of the instructional text.)

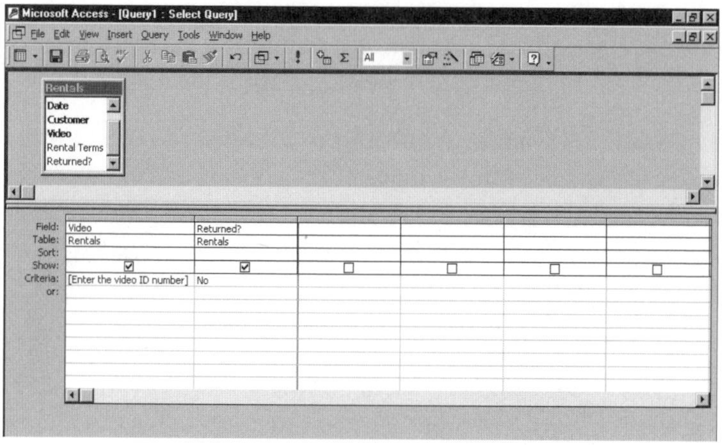

6. Close the query, saving it as *Returned Videos*. Then close the Rentals table.

Now let's create a form based on the query:

Basing a form on a query

1. Select Returned Videos in the Queries list of the Database window, click the New Object button's arrow, and select AutoForm from the drop-down list. Access displays this dialog box:

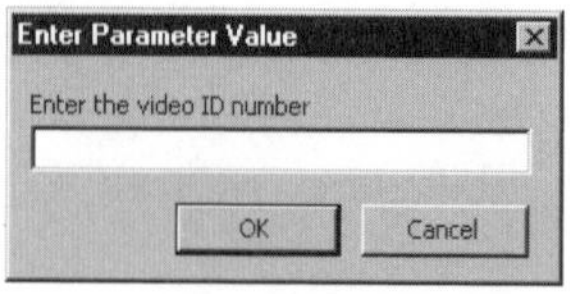

Quick table addition

You can quickly add a table to the query window by dragging the table's name from the Database window to the Query window. Access displays a box with all the table's field names, just as if you had used the Show Table dialog box to add the table.

2. Type *1001* and press Enter. Access closes the dialog box and displays an autoform based on the Returned Videos query.

3. Resize the window to look like this:

4. Click the Returned? check box and close the Form window, saving the form as *Returned Videos*.

5. Now open the Rentals table to be sure that the return information was processed correctly through the Returned Videos query, as shown here:

6. Close the table.

Using Formulas in Queries

Multi-table queries can be useful for accessing fields so that they can then be used in calculations. As you'll see, when you want to use the value of a field in a calculation, you simply enclose the field name in square brackets.

Using field values in calculations

Let's say, for example, that you want to create a form that finds all customers with late videos, displays how late they are, and calculates the fines they owe. The Rentals table doesn't have a field called *Number of Days Late* but it contains the information necessary to calculate this value. First follow these steps to create a query that combines all the necessary fields:

1. With Rentals selected in the Tables list of the Database window, select Query from the New Object drop-down list on the

toolbar. Click OK to open the query in design view, where Rentals has already been added to the Query window.

2. Click the Show Table button on the toolbar and add the Customers and Terms tables to the Query window. Then close the Show Table dialog box. Three tables are now available.

3. Move all the fields from the Rentals table to the QBE grid. Then scroll the grid, move First Name and Last Name from Customers, and move Days and Daily Fine from Terms.

4. In the Criteria row of the Returned? column, type *No* to identify the videos that have not been returned.

5. In the Criteria row of the Date column, type *<(Date()-[Days])*. You are telling Access to calculate whether today's date minus the number of days in the rental period (the value in the Days field) is greater than the date on which the video was rented. If it is, the video is overdue.

In a real database, this query would be reusable because Access adjusts the criteria using the *Date()* command each time you run the query. Before you can test the query on the sample database and see any results, however, you need to change the criteria so that the query will work with our fabricated dates. Here's how to test the query:

1. Change *Date()* in the Criteria row of the Date column to *#7/1/99#* (the # symbols let Access know that this is a date format), so that the criteria is <(#7/1/99#-[Days]).

2. Now run the query. Access identifies these overdue videos:

Relating tables

In the Query window, you can relate two tables that do not have a previously defined relationship. Click and drag from the linking field in the first table box to the linking field in the second table box. Access draws a line between the two fields. Remember, the fields must contain corresponding values for the two tables to be related. To dissolve a relationship, click the line between the two table boxes to select it, and then press the Delete key. Relationships defined in a Query window will not be reflected in the Relationships window—they exist for that query only.

Date	Customer	Video	Terms	Returned?	First Name	Last Name	Day
6/11/99	005	1000 New Release	☐	Ida	Hough	
6/19/99	005	1004 Oldie Weekend	☐	Ida	Hough	
6/24/99	005	1005 One Day Oldie	☐	Ida	Hough	
6/25/99	002	1002 New Release	☐	Ellen	Noy	

Query1 : Select Query

Record: 1 of 4

3. Close the query, saving it as *Late Videos*.

Using Calculated Controls in Forms

You now have half of the job accomplished; you have found the overdue videos, but you have not yet calculated the fines. To complete the job, you need to create a form with some calculated controls. Follow these steps:

1. Select Late Videos from the Queries list of the Database window, select AutoForm from the New Object drop-down list, switch to design view, and maximize the Form window.

2. Rearrange the labels and controls on the form so that it looks like this:

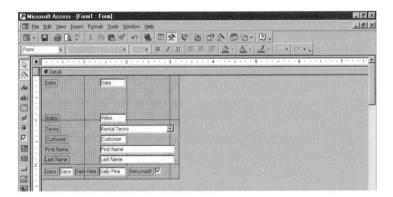

You don't really need the three fields at the bottom of this form, but having them available makes it easier to construct the calculations you need. So instead of deleting them, turn the page to see how to make them invisible.

Adding a group of option buttons

Option buttons and check boxes should be familiar by now, but the difference between them may not be readily apparent. In the Print dialog box, for example, you see round option buttons in the Print Range section for All, Pages, or Selected Records. You must choose one and only one of these option buttons to be able to print. The Collate and Print To File check boxes can be selected singly, together, or not at all. You can add a group of option buttons to a form by clicking the Option Group button on the Toolbox toolbar. After you draw a box in the desired area, Access displays the first Option Group Wizard dialog box. Here, you list the options in the group. Then indicate whether one option is the default and if so, which one. Next specify the values to be assigned to each option for storage purposes and where you want the value stored. Select the type of button, specify how the buttons should look on the form, and assign them a group name. On the form, the buttons appear surrounded by a group box, and only one can be selected at a time. You can add a check box to a form by clicking the Check Box button.

Making fields invisible →

1. Select the labels and controls for Days, Daily Fine, and Returned? by holding down the Shift key and clicking each one.
   Click the Properties button on the toolbar, change the Visible
   property to No, and close the dialog box. (Now the labels and
   controls are visible only in design view.)

2. Click the Text Box button on the Toolbox toolbar and insert
   an unbound text control just below the Date control. Repeat
   this step to insert another text control just below this one.

Changing a label's caption →

3. Now click the Date label, click the Properties button, change
   its Caption property to *Date Rented*, and close the Properties
   dialog box. Then double-click any of the handles around the
   label to resize it.

4. Repeat step 3 to change the Caption properties of the two unbound labels to read *# of Days Late* and *Fines Due.* (You can
   leave the Properties dialog box open and click each label in
   turn.) Then adjust their size and position to look like this:

5. Click the first Unbound control and click the Properties button. On the All tab, change the Name property to *Days Late*,
   and change the Text Align property to Right.

6. Repeat step 5 for the second Unbound control, changing its
   Name property to *Fines*.

   Back in the form, Unbound has not changed, but the names in
   the Object box at the left end of the Formatting toolbar are
   now Days Late and Fines, respectively.

Now let's use the Unbound controls to build formulas to calculate the number of days late and the fine. Try this:

1. Double-click the first Unbound control to display the Properties dialog box, click anywhere in the Control Source property
   edit box, and then click the Build button to display the Expression Builder dialog box shown here:

Specifying the source of
a control's value

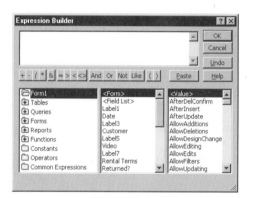

The open Form1 folder represents the unnamed form you are
creating; all its controls and labels are listed in the middle box.
You use these to build a formula that calculates how late the
video is. That formula is then the source of the control's value.

The video's due date is the day it was rented plus the number of days it was rented for. For example, a video rented
on 6/9/99 for two days is due back at South Ridge Video on
6/9/99+2, or 6/11/99. Let's start with this calculation:

2. Double-click the Date field in the middle box and type +.
   Then scroll the middle box and double-click the Days field.
   (The formula is now *[Date]+[Days]*.)

The number of days the video is overdue is the difference between the due date and today's date. Ordinarily, you would
use the Date() function for today's date, but because you are
using fabricated dates for the sample database, let's pretend
that today's date is 7/1/99:

3. Change the formula in the Expression Builder dialog box so
   that it reads as follows:

   =#7/1/99#-([Date]+[Days])

Bound vs. unbound controls

A bound control is linked to a
field in a table. You use bound
controls to display and enter field
values. An unbound control isn't
linked to another database element unless you establish the link.
You can use unbound controls to
display information that is not in
your tables, such as instructions
to the user, or you can establish a
link to an existing database element by clicking the arrow button
in the Control Source edit box of
the Properties dialog box and selecting the element from the drop-
down list.

4. Click OK and then close the Properties dialog box. Access displays the formula in the control.

5. Now repeat step 1 for the second Unbound control. In the Expression Builder dialog box, double-click Daily Fine in the middle box, type *, double-click Days Late (the formula is now *[Daily Fine]*[Days Late]*), and click OK.

6. In the Properties dialog box, change the Format property to Currency, and close the dialog box. The form now looks like the one shown below. (We've enlarged the two calculated controls so that you can see the formulas, but you should make these controls the same size as the Date control above them.)

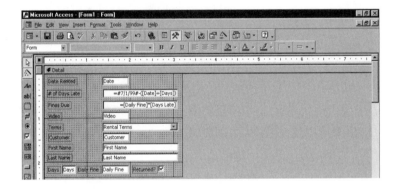

7. Click the Save button and save the form as *Late Videos*. Then switch to form view to see your masterpiece. Here's what the form looks like after we adjusted the size of the controls to correspond better to their contents:

8. Close the Form window.

Using the Total Row in Queries

Access provides a quick and easy way to perform calculations on field values in a query. Using the Total row in the QBE grid, you can find the average, sum, highest value, lowest value, and even the standard deviation and the variance of the values.

Let's say, for example, that Mitch Egan wants to know how many videos were rented on any given day. He doesn't want to know which videos or any other information, just the count of videos rented. Follow these steps to get Mitch what he needs:

1. First add some rental transactions to the Rentals table, simulating several rentals on each of the dates already in the table. (Assign the Terms values randomly, but be sure to click the Returned? check box for the earlier dates.)

2. Create a new query based on the Rentals table and move the Date and Video fields to the QBE grid.

3. Click the Totals button on the toolbar. Access displays a Total row below the Table row, like this:

The Totals button

4. Click the Total row in the Video column and then click the arrow button to display a drop-down list of calculation options.

5. From the drop-down list, select Count. The word *Count* replaces *Group By* in the Total row. (The Group By option tells Access to group similar values in that particular field; see the tip on the next page for definitions of other options.)

The Count function

6. Click the Save button and save the query as *Daily Count*.

7. Run the query. The results for the rental transactions that we entered in the Rentals table in step 1 are shown below. (Your results will be different, depending on the transactions that you entered.)

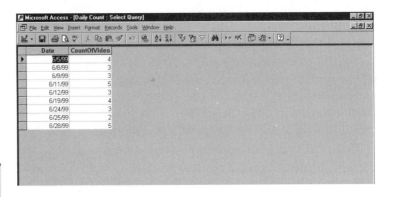

The Count function changes the name of the Video field to CountOfVideo and displays the number of videos that were rented on each day.

8. Close the query and then close the Rentals table.

Using Graphs in Forms

The information in the previous example is useful, but visually bland. Often information can be presented more dramatically using a graph. In Access you can display a graph by embedding it in a form.

Let's create a form that displays a graph of the number of videos rented each day. Follow these steps:

1. Click the Forms icon in the Database window and create a new blank form in design view.

2. Choose Chart from the expanded Insert menu and draw a rectangle on the form. When you release the mouse button, the first Chart Wizard dialog box appears as shown at the top of the facing page. (If a message box asks whether you want to install the Chart Wizard, click Yes and insert the installation CD-ROM if necessary.)

3. Click Queries in the View section, and with Daily Count selected in the list, click Next to display this dialog box:

Specifying the base component

4. Move both the Date and CountOfVideo fields to the Fields For Chart box and click Next to display these graph options:

Specifying the fields

Specifying the graph type

5. Check each graph type in turn and read its description so that you know what's available. Then select the first option in the first row—the 2-D column chart—and click Next to display the dialog box shown here:

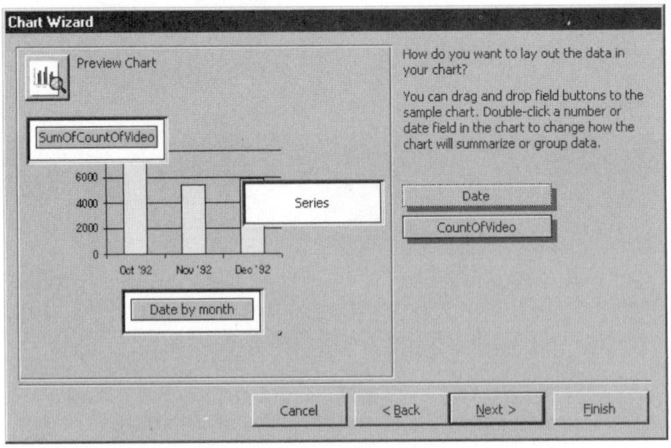

Here, you can preview the graph and go back and change its type if necessary. You can also change the grouping of the fields represented on each axis.

Changing the grouping

6. Double-click the Date By Month control on the preview's x-axis, select Day in the Group dialog box that appears, and click OK. Then click Finish to close the Chart Wizard.

7. Back on the form, Access displays a placeholder graph to designate the area the graph will fill. Enlarge the graph until it almost fills the active grid area of the Detail section.

8. Save the form as *Daily Count* and switch to form view to see the real graph in place, like this:

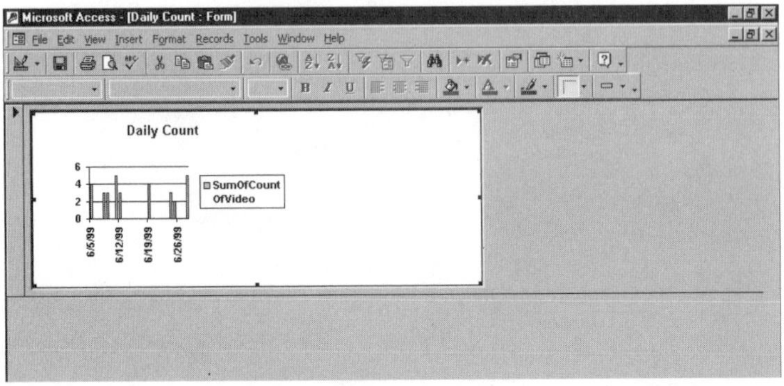

How your graph looks depends on the size of the rectangle and the transactions you entered in the Rentals table.

Graphs often need to be edited significantly before they look the way you want them to. This editing is accomplished in a separate editing environment created by a program called Microsoft Graph. Let's use this program to edit the graph on the form:

← Microsoft Graph

1. Switch to design view, right-click the graph, and from the shortcut menu, choose Chart Object and then Edit. Microsoft Graph opens within Access, replaces the menus and toolbars, and opens the graph's datasheet, which looks like this:

← Editing graphs

Daily Count : Form - Datasheet					
	A	B	C	D	E
	Expr1000	SumOfCountOfVideo			
1	6/5/99	4			
2	6/8/99	3			
3	6/9/99	3			
4	6/11/99	5			

2. Choose Chart Options from the Chart menu and then click the Gridlines tab to display this dialog box:

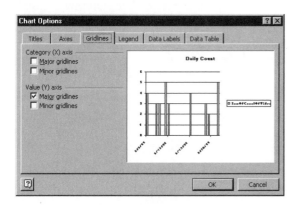

3. In the Value (Y) axis section, click the Major Gridlines check box to deselect it, and then click OK to remove the gridlines.

4. Click any of the graph's blue columns. (These columns plot the first series of data—in this case, the only series of data.)

Microsoft Graph

Microsoft Graph comes with Access and Microsoft Office 2000. You can use Graph as a stand-alone program, but you will generally use it in conjunction with Access (or with the other Office programs). The Graph program has its own Help system, so if you are interested in exploring its capabilities further, check out the topics available in its Help feature.

Handles appear on all the columns to indicate that they are selected.

The More Buttons button and the Fill Color button

5. Click the More Buttons button at the right end of Graph's Standard toolbar, click the arrow to the right of the Fill Color button, and select yellow from the drop-down palette.

The Chart Type button

6. Click the arrow to the right of the Chart Type button, and select the different types in turn. (If you select a format that is incompatible with the data, Graph displays a message box.) Finish by reselecting the 2-D column type (the first option in the third row).

Deleting the legend

7. Because this graph is very simple, you don't really need the legend. Click it once to select it and then press the Delete key.

8. Since you know there are several dates to display along the y-axis of the graph, widen the chart until it almost fills the Detail section.

Changing the axis scale

9. You can see the daily count values for every other day. Tell Graph to show every day on the y-axis by right-clicking it, choosing Format Axis from the shortcut menu, and changing the Major Unit entry on the Scale tab from 2 to 1. Click OK.

Types of graphs

Listed below are the main types of graphs you can create in Access. The type of graph you select should take into account the kind of data you want to display.

- **Bar graphs.** Ideal for displaying the values of several items at a single point in time
- **Column graphs.** The best choice for displaying the variations in the value of a single item over time
- **Line graphs.** Often used to show variations in the values of more than one item over time
- **Area graphs.** Similar to line graphs except that they plot multiple data series as cumulative layers with different colors, patterns, or shades
- **Pie graphs.** Good for displaying the percentages of an item that can be assigned to the item's components
- **Scatter graphs.** Great for plotting two values to see if there is any correlation between them
- **Combination graphs.** Can show two different types of graphs at once; for example, combinations of line and bar graphs, or bar and area graphs
- **3-D graphs.** Useful for displaying data with two or more variables; available for these types of graphs: line, bar, column, area, and pie

Other available types of graphs include doughnut, radar, bubble, surface, cylinder, and pyramid. For more information, see Graph's Help feature.

10. Click outside the graphic and datasheet to close Microsoft Graph and return to design view. Then enlarge the Details section and the graph to better fit the new scale. (You may have to reopen Microsoft Graph by double-clicking the graph in design view in order to get its size just right.)

11. Switch to form view to check the display of the graph. Then, if necessary, switch back to design view, and enlarge the graph's frame. (Drag the handle in the bottom right corner down and to the right until you can see the entire graph.) When you finish adjusting the graph, it looks like this in form view:

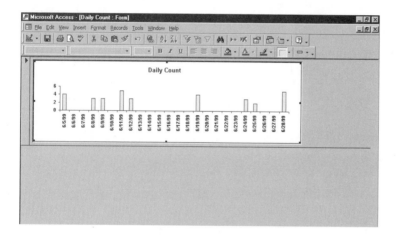

12. Close the form, saving your changes.

A full tour of Microsoft Graph is beyond the scope of this book. If you are familiar with other Microsoft applications, most of the options are fairly intuitive, and you can always turn to Graph's Help feature if you get stuck.

Well, you made it through our examples of some of the more advanced uses of forms and queries. Use these examples as springboards for your own ideas, and you'll soon discover an infinite variety of ways to retrieve and display information.

6

Database Maintenance and Management

After a discussion of updating switchboards, we deal with the maintenance of a database and how to use action queries to manipulate multiple records simultaneously. Then we briefly describe how to secure a database that has multiple users.

Almost any database needs updating and maintaining if it is to remain useful. A database that is accessed by multiple users, such as students or customers, also needs to be secured to prevent accidental or deliberate corruption.

Tasks performed and concepts covered:

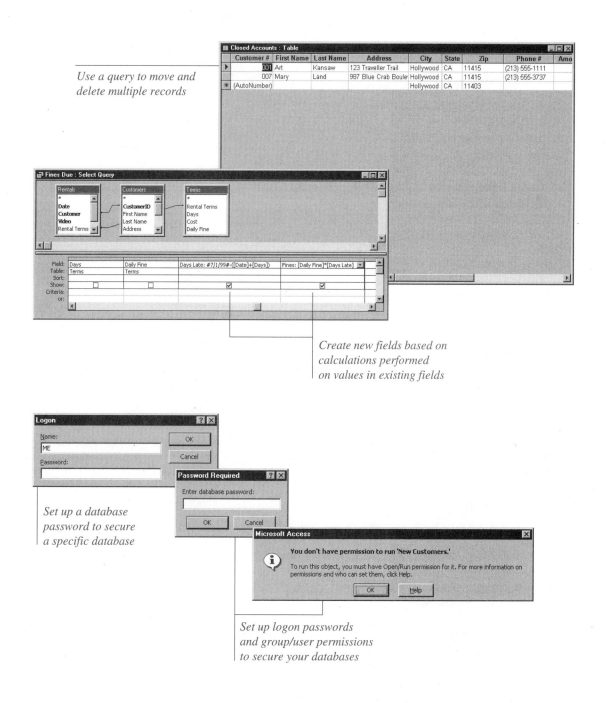

Use a query to move and delete multiple records

Create new fields based on calculations performed on values in existing fields

Set up a database password to secure a specific database

Set up logon passwords and group/user permissions to secure your databases

In this chapter, we discuss issues relating to ongoing maintenance of databases and managing them from a security point of view. We start by showing you how to maintain a switchboard, modifying it so that it always reflects the changing contents of its database. Then you look at ways to keep databases up-to-date and how to build in the flexibility to meet future needs. Up until now, you have dealt with only one record at a time and one user at a time. In the real world, however, you generally work with several records and several users. You'll get a feeling for how to manipulate multiple records in the first part of the chapter, and we'll talk about how to handle multiple users in the second part.

More About Switchboards

Since creating the switchboard in Chapter 3, you have added several forms, queries, and reports to the South Ridge Video database. You could add all of these objects to the main switchboard, but it would then be cluttered and possibly confusing for new users. To avoid this problem, you can link a series of switchboards to the main switchboard to lead new users through various options, much like the folders and subfolders used in the Windows environment.

As a demonstration, let's construct a switchboard containing all the reports in the database and link it to the main switchboard. Follow these steps to create a new switchboard:

Modifying a switchboard

When modifying a switchboard created by the Database Wizard, always use the Switchboard Manager rather than trying to make the modifications in design view. A switchboard form works by using entries in the Switchboard Items table that describe what the buttons on the form display and do. If you try to make design changes to the switchboard form, the application may stop working.

1. With the South Ridge Video Database window open on your screen, choose Database Utilities and then Switchboard Manager from the Tools menu.

2. In the Switchboard Manager dialog box, click New and name the new switchboard *Reports Switchboard*. Click OK.

3. Select Reports Switchboard and click Edit.

4. To add an item to this switchboard, click New in the Edit Switchboard Page dialog box. Type *Customer Mailing Labels* in the Text edit box, change the Command setting to Open Report, and change the Report setting to Customer Mailing Labels. Then click OK.

5. Repeat step 4 to create a switchboard item called *Movies By Rating* that opens the Movies report.

6. Close the Edit Switchboard Page dialog box.

    Now you've created a switchboard, but you have yet to link it to your main switchboard. Here are the steps:

1. Select Main Switchboard, click Edit, and then click New in the Edit Switchboard Page dialog box.

    Linking switchboards

2. In the Edit Switchboard Item dialog box, type *Print reports* in the Text edit box. Select Go To Switchboard as the Command setting and then select Reports Switchboard as the Switchboard setting. Click OK.

3. Click Close twice to close the Edit Switchboard Page dialog box and then the Switchboard Manager dialog box.

    Now test the new switchboard:

1. Move to the Forms list in the Database window, select Switchboard, and click Open. Access opens the Main Switchboard (see page 84), where a new Print Reports item is listed.

    Testing the links

2. Click the Print Reports check box. Access jumps to the new switchboard, where the reports are listed as shown here:

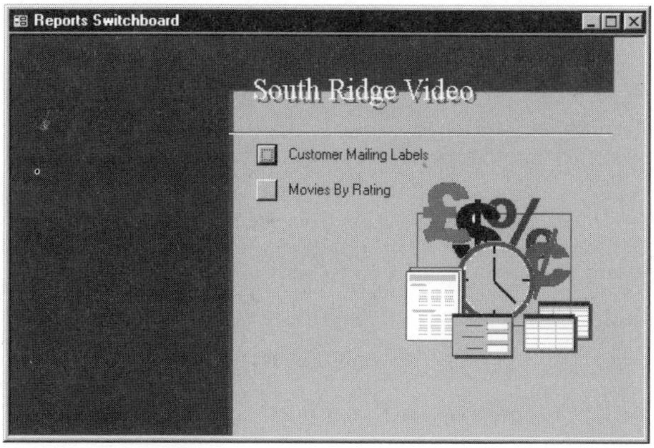

3. Click one of the reports to jump directly to its window. Then close that window and click the other report to test its link.

4. Close the Report window and then close the switchboard.

Working with More than One Record

Maintaining a database would be an arduous task if you were limited to working with single records. Fortunately, Access provides several ways to perform actions on multiple records.

Creating New Tables with Queries

Sometimes you will want to create a new table using some of the records in an existing table. You could reenter all the records in a new table; or you could save the existing table with a new name and then delete the records you don't want. A third possibility is to use a query to extract the records you want into a datasheet that you then turn into the new table.

Let's look at an example. In Chapter 5, you used a form to calculate the fines due on late videos. Suppose you now realize you need that information in table format to be able to generate reports. Let's create a Fines Due query and then convert the query datasheet to a table. Here are the steps:

1. In the Queries list of the Database window, select the Late Videos query and open it in design view.

2. Choose Save As from the File menu and save the query with the name *Fines Due*.

3. Select and delete the First Name and Last Name columns.

4. Click the Show boxes of the Video, Rental Terms, Returned?, Days, and Daily Fine fields to tell Access not to display these fields in the query datasheet.

Calculations in queries

5. In the Field row of the next blank column, type the following formula, which is the same as the one used to calculate the number of days late in the Late Videos form (see page 137):

#7/1/99#-([Date]+[Days])

6. Press Enter. Then check that the Show box in this column is selected so that Access will include the results of the formula in the query datasheet.

7. Notice that Access has entered *Expr1* in front of the formula as the name of the field that will hold the formula results. Replace this name with *Days Late* (leave the colon).

Naming the calculated field

8. Repeat steps 5 through 7 to enter the following formula in the next available column:

Fines: [Daily Fine][Days Late]*

9. Double-click the right border of the thin gray box above the Field row of the Days Late field to widen the column to fit its contents. Repeat this step for the Fines field. Here's what the formulas look like:

Widening QBE grid columns

	Fines Due : Select Query			
	Rentals	Customers	Terms	
	*	*	*	
	Date	CustomerID	Rental Terms	
	Customer	First Name	Days	
	Video	Last Name	Cost	
	Rental Terms	Address	Daily Fine	

Field:	Days	Daily Fine	Days Late: #7/1/99#-([Date]+[Days])	Fines: [Daily Fine]*[Days Late]
Table:	Terms	Terms		
Sort:				
Show:	☐	☐	☑	☑
Criteria:				
or:				

Now tell Access to turn the results of the query into a new table. You do this by changing the type of the query, like this:

1. Click the arrow to the right of the Query Type button on the toolbar and select Make Table Query from the drop-down list. Access displays this dialog box:

The Query Type button

Make Table	? ✕
Make New Table	OK
Table Name:	Cancel
● Current Database	
○ Another Database:	
File Name:	

2. Type *Overdue* in the Table Name edit box and press Enter. (The new table's name can't be the same as the query name.)

3. Now run the query. Access displays the dialog box shown on the next page. (Your number of rows may be different.)

4. Click Yes to create the table, click the Save button to save the query, and then close the Query window. In the Database window, Access identifies the make table query with a distinctive icon.

For peace of mind, let's verify that Access successfully created the table:

1. Click the Tables icon, select the Overdue table, and open it in datasheet view.

2. To display the Fines field values as dollars, click the View button to switch to design view. Click anywhere in the Fines field, set its Format property to Currency, and save your changes. Then click the View button again to see these results, which reflect the rentals you entered in Chapter 5:

Date	Customer	Days Late	Fines
6/24/99	6	6	$60.00
6/25/99	2	5	$50.00
6/28/99	3	2	$20.00
6/11/99	3	19	$190.00
6/19/99	3	11	$55.00
6/24/99	1	6	$60.00
6/28/99	2	2	$10.00
6/28/99	6	2	$20.00
6/28/99	1	2	$20.00
6/28/99	8	2	$10.00

Record: |◄| |◄| | 1 | |►| |►|| |►*| of 10

3. Close the Table window.

Updating Records with Queries

From time to time, you may want to change a value in several records in a table. For example, if you assign a new salesperson

Caution: rerunning make table queries

Make table queries can be very useful, but be aware of the difference between make table and append queries (discussed on page 157). If you run a make table query and the table already exists, the query will overwrite the existing table, whereas an append query will add its results to an existing table.

to a sales area, you may need to change the salesperson's name in records in a Customers or Invoices table.

For demonstration purposes, suppose Hollywood is assigned a new zip code, and you need to update the Customers table to reflect the change. You could update each record in turn, but an easier way is to use an update query. Follow these steps:

1. With Customers selected in the Tables list of the Database window, choose Query from the New Object button's drop-down list and click OK to open a new query based on the Customers table in design view.

2. Double-click the PostalCode field to add it to the QBE grid.

3. Select Update Query from the Query Type button's drop-down list. Access changes the select query to an update query and adds an Update To row to the QBE grid. ←──── Specifying an update query

4. In the Update To row of the PostalCode column, type *11415*. ←──── The Update To row

5. In the Criteria row, type *11403*, and press Enter. The query looks like this:

6. Run the query. Access advises you of the number of records to be updated in this dialog box:

7. Click Yes to complete the changes and then close the query without saving it.

Caution: leaving the Criteria row blank

In an update query, if you enter information in the Update To row but leave the Criteria row blank, Access assumes that you want to make the change no matter what the existing field value is. The result is that Access updates every record in the table. So be careful when you run update queries!

8. Open the Customers table, where all the records for customers who live in Hollywood now have the new zip code. (Obviously, you will need to update the PostalCode field's Default Value property as well.)

For a small table, it may be much faster to make the changes manually. For large tables, using an update query is definitely faster and ensures that all the affected records are changed.

Moving Records with Queries

There are a few things you have not considered in the South Ridge Video database. One is what to do when a customer closes an account. If you keep all the customer records, both active and inactive, in the Customers table, the table may soon become too large to work with on a daily basis. Also, you may want to keep additional information about closed customer accounts, such as whether they owe any fines.

One solution is to create a Closed Accounts table in the database and then move inactive customers from the Customers table to the Closed Accounts table. To work through this example, you need to add a Closed field to the Customers table:

1. Open the Customers table in design view, and add a Closed field below PhoneNumber. Set the data type to Yes/No, type *No* as the Default Value property, and save your changes.

2. Switch to datasheet view, click the Closed check boxes for Art Kansaw and Mary Land, and close the table.

Now you're ready to create the Closed Accounts table:

1. With Customers selected in the Database window, click the Copy button on the toolbar and then click the Paste button. Access displays this dialog box:

2. In the Table Name edit box, type *Closed Accounts*, click the Structure Only option, and click OK. Access adds the new table to the list in the Database window.

3. Open the Closed Accounts table in design view and delete the Closed field by clicking its row selector and pressing Delete. (All the records in this table are for closed accounts so this field is redundant.)

4. Create a new Amount Due field, set the data type to Number, and set the Format property to Currency.

5. Close the table, saving your changes when prompted.

You can now move the closed records from the Customers table to the Closed Accounts table. This is a two-step, append-and-delete operation, as you'll see if you follow the steps in the next two sections.

Appending Records

You now have a table in which to store the records for the customers that are inactive. Follow these steps to move these records to the Closed Accounts table:

1. Select the Customers table in the Tables list of the Database window, select Query from the New Object button's drop-down list, and click OK to open the query in design view.

2. Add all the fields from the Customers box to the QBE grid by double-clicking the Customers title bar, pointing to the selected fields, and then dragging the pointer to the first column of the QBE grid.

3. Type *Yes* in the Criteria row of the Closed column.

4. Now select Append Query from the Query Type button's drop-down list. Access displays this dialog box:

Specifying an append query

5. Click the arrow to the right of the Table Name edit box, select *Closed Accounts* as the name of the table to which you want to append the results of the query, and click OK.

6. Run the query. Access tells you that it will append two rows:

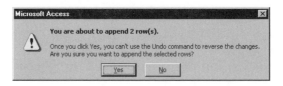

7. Click Yes to proceed with the query and then close it, saving it as *Append Closed Accounts*.

8. Now open the Closed Accounts table to verify that it contains the two closed records, as shown here:

Crosstab queries

Crosstab queries are a useful way of displaying data in a grid format—similar to a pivot table in spreadsheets—so that the data is easier to compare. For example, a crosstab query could be used to compare the number of rentals for each customer, grouped by rental type. To set up a crosstab query, you can select the Crosstab Query Wizard from the New Query dialog box or you can create a new query for the appropriate tables, add the fields you want to the QBE grid, and then select Crosstab Query from the Query Type drop-down list to add a Crosstab row and a Total row to the QBE grid. Use the options in the Crosstab row to determine which fields are rows, columns, and values. Then set up the functions you need in the Total row and run the query. The datasheet is displayed as a grid with the row and column headings you specified in the Crosstab row.

Customer #	First Name	Last Name	Address	City	State	Zip	Phone #	Amo
001	Art	Kansaw	123 Traveller Trail	Hollywood	CA	11415	(213) 555-1111	
007	Mary	Land	987 Blue Crab Boule	Hollywood	CA	11415	(213) 555-3737	
(AutoNumber)				Hollywood	CA	11403		

9. Close the Table window.

You can run this query whenever you need to append records from the Customers table to the Closed Accounts table. You can then check the Overdue table and enter any fines owed by customers with closed accounts.

Deleting Records

You have copied the closed records to the Closed Accounts table, but the records still exist in the Customers table. You could easily delete them individually because there are only two. But what if you want to delete many records that are scattered throughout the table? A better technique is to set up a query to delete the records for you. Follow these steps:

1. Create a new query based on the Customers table and open it in design view.

2. Add all the fields in the Customers box to the QBE grid.

3. Select Delete Query from the Query Type button's drop-down list. Access adds a Delete row to the QBE grid with Where in each column.

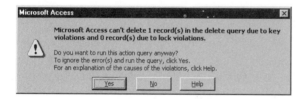

Specifying a delete query

4. Type *Yes* in the Criteria row of the Closed column to delete all the records where the Closed field value is Yes.

5. Save the query as *Delete Closed Accounts*.

6. Without changing any of the entries in the grid, run the query. When Access advises you that two records will be deleted, click Yes to proceed. Access then displays this message:

The results demonstrate how Access safeguards your databases by preventing you from introducing errors. Access does not tell you exactly what the problem is, but it does tell you that deleting one of the records will produce *key violations*, meaning that the record is referenced by at least one record in a related table. Even if you click Yes in this dialog box, the offending record will not be deleted. Follow these steps to see where the problem lies:

1. Click No, and then click the Database Window button on the toolbar.

Pivot tables

If you are familiar with Excel and would like to display your data in a pivot table, an alternative to creating a crosstab query is to create a form by selecting Pivot-Table Wizard in the New Form dialog box. Access then walks you through the steps of creating a pivot table. Clicking a button on the newly created pivot-table form opens Excel so that you can edit the pivot table directly. (The underlying data is not affected.)

Tracking relationships

2. Click the Relationships button on the toolbar to display the relationships you've established between the tables of the South Ridge Video database, as shown here:

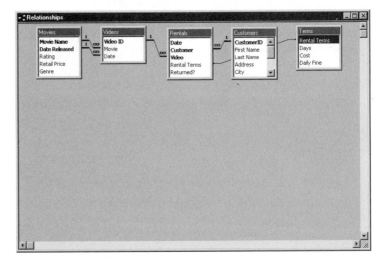

The Customers table has only one relationship linking CustomerID to Customer in the Rentals table, so this must be the relationship that is causing the key violation. (If you instructed Access to create relationships for you when you were experimenting with sub-datasheets on page 112, your window may show more relationships.)

Displaying relationship
properties

3. Right-click the thin part of the line between Customer ID and Customer and choose Edit Relationship from the shortcut menu to display this dialog box:

The relationship between CustomerID and Customer is One-To-Many with referential integrity enforced. Because of the referential integrity, you have a tough decision to make:

- If you turn off the Enforce Referential Integrity option, Access will allow you to enter Customer values in the Rentals table that do not correspond to CustomerID values in the Customers table. For example, a clerk would be able to rent a movie to customer 3000 when no such customer exists.

- If you want to leave referential integrity in force, you could remove all records from the Rentals table involving the customer whose record you are trying to delete from the Customers table. (You might want to create a Closed Accounts Rental History table and store these records there. However, compiling rental information would then be more difficult. If Mrs. Egan wanted to know how many videos were rented in a given month, you would need to remember to include these closed rental transactions in the calculation.)

There is no easy answer to this problem. The solution depends on which is more important to the Egans: complete rental information in one table or a built-in check on the Customer values entered by the clerks. For this example, let's turn off the Enforce Referential Integrity option and assume that the Egans train their clerks well:

4. Deselect the Enforce Referential Integrity check box in the Edit Relationships dialog box, click OK, and then close the Relationships window.

5. Click the title bar of the Delete Closed Accounts window to activate the query and then rerun the query, clicking Yes to delete the two closed records.

6. Close the Query window.

Databases are rarely static. As you have seen, you can use queries to efficiently maintain a database by dealing with multiple records or entire tables at once.

Dealing with More than One User

Databases created for small businesses and the home often have only one user. However, in large businesses, one or two people usually create and maintain the database, but many others use the database to update and retrieve information.

Database replication

If you need to create copies of a database for use at multiple sites (for example, branch offices), you can use database replication to ensure that although each site works on its own copy, any changes can all be incorporated back into the original version. Database replication is beyond the scope of this book. If you need to use replication, consult the Help feature.

South Ridge Video, for example, may have several clerks who use the database but are not allowed to change its design or structure. Because a database is only as good as the integrity of its information, securing the database is often critical, but it can also be a headache.

Setting a Password for a Database

The simplest method of securing a database that won't be replicated is to assign a password for opening it. This method is most useful when only a few people use the database and each is trustworthy and knowledgable enough to have full access to all database components. Let's assign a password now:

1. Close the South Ridge Video database. If you are asked whether you want to empty the Clipboard, click Yes.

Temporarily locking out other users

2. Click the Open button on the toolbar to display the Open dialog box. With South Ridge Video selected, click the arrow to the right of the Open button and select the Open Exclusive option from the drop-down list.

3. Choose Security and then Set Database Password from the Tools menu to display this dialog box:

4. In both the Password and Verify edit boxes, type *opensesame* and click OK. (Passwords are case sensitive, so keep it all lowercase.)

The Exclusive option

When you open a database with the Exclusive option selected, you shut out any other users of the database while you have it open. This option is very useful on networked computers, but it's not as important to single computer users.

5. Close the database and then try to reopen it. Access displays this dialog box:

6. Type *opensesame* in the edit box and press Enter.

Setting Security for Several Users

Security in Access is a complicated affair, based on a system of *groups* to which password-protected *user accounts* are assigned. By default, two groups are created by Access: *Admins* and *Users*. Admins is an elite group, reserved for database administrators with omnipotent powers; Users is not so picky. In fact, all accounts are automatically assigned to Users as well as to more specific groups. By default, one user account is set up with the name *Admin* and is assigned to both the Admins and Users groups. When you start Access, the program assumes that you are this Admin user, logs you on without requiring a password, and gives you unrestricted power over any database you create or open, unless that database has been secured.

◄───── The default groups

◄───── The default user

Securing a database involves several steps, and any missteps can produce unexpected results. We'll walk you through the process (and then walk you back), but here's a brief overview of what you need to do:

- Use the Workgroup Administrator to create a new workgroup information file, which identifies groups and their members.

- Add a new user to the Admins group.

- Remove the Admin user from Admins so that Admin is a member of the Users group only, and then assign a password to the Admin user.

- Restart Access as the new user.

- Create a new database and remove all Users group permissions for each object type in that database.

- Import the objects from the original database into the new database.

- Create groups and users as necessary and assign group and user permissions that control what a user can do.

Seem like a lot of work? It is, but the result—a controlled database environment—is worth it if your data is critical to

Deleting database passwords

You can delete a database password—for example, the *open-sesame* password you created for the South Ridge Video database. Open the database by displaying the Open dialog box, selecting the database you want to open, and then clicking the Open Exclusive option in the Open drop-down list. Then enter the password. Next choose Security and then Unset Database Password from the Tools menu. Type the current password in the Password edit box and then click OK. You will no longer need to enter a password to open the database.

your company's operations. In the next section, we'll explain the steps in more detail.

Caution!

A note of caution: The workgroup information file, groups, and user accounts operate at the program level, not at the database level. Users identify themselves when the program starts, not when a database opens. Unless you have complete control of Access on your system, be sure to consult with other program users before you begin changing this level of security.

Creating a Secure Workgroup

The workgroup
information file

Access stores all information about groups, users, and passwords in a separate file that is stored in the main Access folder. When the program was installed, Access automatically associated the user name and the company name with this file. As you can imagine, this combination is fairly easy for someone attempting to break into a database to discover. So Access won't let you change any of the program's security information until you customize this file and give it a password. Follow these steps to make this change:

1. Close Access. Open Windows Explorer, navigate to the C:\Program Files\Microsoft Office\Office folder, and find the MS Access Workgroup Administrator shortcut.

The Workgroup Administrator
program

2. Double-click the shortcut to start the Workgroup Administrator program, as shown here:

3. Click Create to display the dialog box shown at the top of the facing page.

4. Type your name and organization. In the Workgroup ID edit box, type a password you will easily recall. It can be any combination of up to 20 letters and numbers, and it is case sensitive. Important: Before you click OK, be sure to write down all the information from this dialog box. If you ever need to recreate this file, there is no way to retrieve this information from your computer.   ← **Important!**

5. Click OK to display this dialog box:

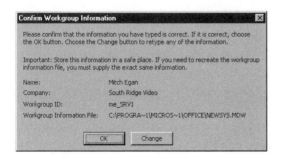

6. Change the name of the file to something memorable and click OK. (We chose NEWSYS.MDW. You can leave the filename as SYSTEM.MDW if you want.) Access then displays this confirmation:

7. If everything looks correct, click OK. Then click OK to close the confirmation message box, and click Exit to quit the

Splitting a database

Another useful tool for managing a database accessed by multiple users on a network is the Database Splitter. This tool separates a database so that its tables are stored in one file and its forms, queries, and reports are stored in another. Users on the network can then create their own forms, queries, and reports to extract information from the database's tables, which remain intact in their own file, but cannot be changed. To split a database, choose Database Utilities and then Database Splitter from the Tools menu and follow the instructions presented by the Database Splitter Wizard.

Workgroup Administrator program. Finally, close Windows Explorer.

Behind the scenes, Access records in the Windows Registry the name of the workgroup information file to be used whenever you start Access.

Creating User Accounts

Now that you have taken this first security measure, Access will allow you to create new groups and users. Let's start by creating an Owner account in the existing Admins group. Follow these steps:

1. Start Access and open the South Ridge Video database, entering the *opensesame* password when prompted.

2. From the Tools menu, choose Security and then User And Group Accounts. Access displays this dialog box:

Names, personal IDs, and passwords

The personal ID (PID) you enter in the New User/Group dialog box is combined with the name you enter to create an encrypted security ID (SID), which Access stores in the workgroup information file and uses to identify each account. You need to accurately record each account's name and PID so that you can recreate the account if the workgroup information file becomes damaged. After you create an account, you assign it a password. This password is exactly what you would expect it to be: a unique identifier associated with the user's name for purposes of logging on to Access.

3. Click New in the User section to display this dialog box:

4. Type *Owner* in both the Name edit box and the Personal ID edit box and click OK.

By default, the Owner account is listed only as a member of the all-purpose Users group, which you will usually want to have the most restricted access to databases. You want the Owner account to have unlimited access, so you need to add it to the Admins group, which by default is unrestricted.

5. With Admins selected in the Available Groups section, click the Add button. Admins is added to the list that defines which groups the Owner account is a member of.

Adding users to groups

6. You want Owner to be the only account with unlimited access to databases, so select Admin from the Name drop-down list in the User section, and remove it from the Admins group by clicking Remove with the Admins group selected in the Member Of list.

Removing users from groups

7. Currently, the Admin account has no password. To create a password, click the Change Logon Password tab and type *Ridge* in the New Password and Verify edit boxes. Then click OK to close the User And Group Accounts dialog box.

Changing passwords

8. Close Access completely, saving any changes if prompted.

The advantage of activating security at the program level is that users enter their passwords only once, and Access passes their security information to any databases they open.

Creating a Secure Database

The current South Ridge Video database is "owned" by its creator, the default Admin user. You need to create a secure version of this database that can be modified only by the Owner user. (From now on, you will only be using the secure version of the database so that you can return to the original South Ridge Video database if you make any mistakes.) Follow these steps:

1. Restart Access and double-click South Ridge Video to open it. This dialog box appears:

Good and bad passwords

Passwords that are easy to decipher can give users a false sense of security. Birth dates and social security numbers are obvious examples of bad passwords. Using common words is also inappropriate, however, because some "hackers" use computer programs that run through entire dictionaries, trying each word until they find the password. A good rule for passwords is to use letters and symbols to form nonsensical words, always longer than four characters. Try substituting + for N, $ for S, or @ for A to form passwords such as *$uperm@+*, *$ale$*, and *ope+$e$ame*.

You would see this same dialog box no matter which database you tried to open because security is set at the program level rather than for individual database files.

2. Type *Owner* in the Name edit box, leave the Password edit box blank, and then click OK. (We don't assign passwords to the accounts we create in our examples. However, in practice, you probably would want to password-protect all accounts.)

3. Type *opensesame* in the Password edit box.

4. Click the New button on the toolbar (not the window's toolbar) and create a blank database called *Secure South Ridge Video*.

Having created the database, you need to specify who can do what with it. The right to perform a particular activity is called a *permission*, and you can grant permissions to individual users or to an entire group of users. A user always has the permissions assigned to his or her group; you can't take any away. But you can give a user more permissions than those assigned to his or her group. This setup is flexible yet efficient, because you can usually make changes in one place—at the group level—instead of having to work with several different user accounts. Here's a list of the available permissions:

Permissions

This Permission...	Allows Users to...
Open/Run	Open databases, forms, and reports and run macros
Read Data	View data in tables and queries
Update Data	View and modify data but not insert or delete data in tables and queries
Insert Data	View and insert data but not modify or delete it in tables and queries
Delete Data	View and delete data but not modify or insert it in tables and queries
Read Design	View tables, queries, forms, reports, macros, and modules in design view
Modify Design	View, change the design of, and delete tables, queries, forms, reports, macros, and modules
Administer	Set passwords, replicate, and change startup properties of databases; work with objects and data in tables, queries, forms, reports, macros, and modules in any way; assign permissions if necessary

Let's remove the default permissions of the Users group:

1. Choose Security and then User And Group Permissions from the Tools menu to display this dialog box:

For each object in a database, you can assign any of the applicable permissions to a user or group. A check mark signifies that the permission has been granted.

2. Click the Groups option and select Users in the User/Group Name list box. As you can see, this group starts with unlimited access. You must therefore tell Access what members of this group *can't* do, rather than what they can do, by unchecking boxes.

Removing the Users group permissions

3. With Table selected in the Object Type box and New Tables/Queries selected in the Object Name list, deselect all the check boxes in the Permissions section, and click Apply. (Notice that clicking certain check boxes, such as Read Data, clears several check boxes at once.)

4. Change the Object Type to Form, deselect all the permissions, and click Apply.

5. Repeat step 4 for all the database components in the Object Type drop-down list except Database (at the top of the list). Then click OK.

Who has what permissions?

If you check a particular user's permissions in the User And Group Permissions dialog box, it may appear that the user has no permissions when in fact he or she has all the permissions assigned to his or her group. Always check the group's permissions first, because the user can have more permissions than the group but not fewer permissions.

Let's import the components of the unsecure South Ridge Video database into the new secure database. Try this:

Importing database
components

1. Choose Get External Data and then Import from the File menu to display the Import dialog box. Select South Ridge Video and click Import. Type the *opensesame* password when prompted and click OK. This dialog box appears:

2. Click Select All on the Tables tab, then click the Queries tab, and click Select All again. Repeat this step to select all the objects on all the tabs, and then click OK.

3. When prompted, save the Customers data access page with the name *Secure Customers*.

You now have a secure version of the South Ridge Video database that can be accessed only by the Owner user.

Creating Groups

The next step is to create groups for the users you want to be able to work with the database. Only members of the Admins group can create groups. For this example, let's create a group called *Clerks* that is not as restricted as the Users group:

1. Choose Security and then User And Group Accounts from the Tools menu.

2. Click the Groups tab and then click New. Create a group called *Clerks* with a Personal ID of *Cashiers*, and click OK.

Having created the Clerks group, let's add a couple of user accounts to it. Here are the steps:

1. Click the Users tab and then click New.

Importing databases

Access 2000 can import databases created by several other programs. Simply choose Get External Data and then Import from the File menu, select a format, locate the database file, and click Import. Depending on the format you've selected, Access may use a wizard to obtain the additional information it needs to convert and display the file.

2. In the New User/Group dialog box, type *Al Bammer* under both Name and Personal ID and then click OK.

3. Add Al Bammer to the Clerks group by selecting Clerks in the Available Groups list and clicking the Add button.

4. Repeat steps 1 and 2 to add a user called *Minnie Soder* to the Clerks group and then click OK.

   You now have a new group with two user accounts assigned to it. Next you need to tell Access what types of activities these users can perform. Follow these steps to set the permissions for the new Clerks group:

1. Choose Security and then User And Group Permissions from the Tools menu to display the User And Group Permissions dialog box.

   Assigning group permissions

2. To display a list of existing groups, click the Groups option in the User/Group Name list box, and then select Clerks.

3. With Table selected as the Object Type, select Rentals in the Object Name list, click the Read Data, Update Data, and Insert Data check boxes in the Permissions section, and click Apply.

4. Because the Rentals table is related to the Customers, Movies, Terms, and Videos tables, select each of them in turn and assign the Read Data permission.

5. Change the Object Type to Form, select Rentals in the Object Name list, click the Open/Run check box, and click Apply.

   Members of the Clerks group can now work with the Rentals table and the corresponding form. But suppose Al Bammer is also allowed to open new customer accounts. Here's how to give him permissions that the rest of his group doesn't have:

1. In the User And Group Permissions dialog box, click the Users option and select Al Bammer from the User/Group Name list box.

   Assigning user permissions

2. Change the Object Type to Table and select Customers. Click the Read Data, Update Data, and Insert Data check boxes, and then click Apply.

3. Change the Object Type to Form, select New Customers, click the Open/Run check box, click Apply, and then click OK to close the dialog box.

Now follow these steps to test the new group's security:

Testing security

1. Quit Access, restart the program, and then open the Secure South Ridge Video database, logging on as *Minnie Soder* with no password.

2. Click the Forms icon, open the Rentals form, and then close it.

3. Now try to open the New Customers form. Because Minnie Soder doesn't have permission to work with this form, Access displays this dialog box:

The permissions for the Clerks group are obviously in effect, controlling the Access activities of this group of users.

4. Click OK to close the dialog box.

5. Quit Access and then restart the program.

6. Open the Secure South Ridge Video database, log on as *Al Bammer* with no password, and test this user's permissions.

Removing Security Settings

Before we end this chapter, we'll show you how to undo your security measures so that you can use Access in the normal way. Follow these steps:

1. Quit and restart Access, and then open the Secure South Ridge Video database, logging on as *Owner*.

2. Choose Security and then User And Group Accounts from the Tools menu.

The User-Level Security Wizard

In order for you to better understand the process for creating a secure database, we have taken you through all the steps manually. However, once you have a good grasp of database security, you may want to explore the User-Level Security Wizard. To create a secure database using the wizard, complete the first four bulleted steps listed on page 163. Then choose Security and User-Level Security Wizard from the Tools menu to activate the wizard. When you have completed the wizard's dialog boxes, Access takes care of the fifth and sixth bulleted steps. Access also encrypts the database. You then need to complete the final bulleted step as usual.

3. On the Users tab, delete Al Bammer and Minnie Soder by selecting them from the Name list and clicking the Delete button. Click Yes to confirm the deletions. Then add Admin to the Admins group and click Clear Password.

Deleting users

4. On the Groups tab, delete the Clerks group. Click Yes to confirm the deletion. Then click OK to close the dialog box.

Deleting groups

5. Choose Security and then User And Group Permissions from the Tools menu.

6. Click the Change Owner tab and make sure that Admin appears in the New Owner edit box. For each Object Type except Database, select all the items in the Object list and click Change Owner. (To select all the items, click the first item, hold down the Shift key, and click the last item on the list.)

Changing the database owner

7. Click the Permissions tab and select Admin in the User/Group Name list box. For each Object Type, select all the items in the Object Name list and click the Administer check box twice to ensure that full permissions are assigned to the Admin user. Then click Apply. When you are finished, click OK.

Assigning full permissions

8. Quit Access and restart the program. Because the Admins group now includes an Admin user with no password, Access automatically logs you into the program as that user. (Now you can see why the first security measure was to create a new user account in the Admins group and remove the Admin user from that group!)

9. Open the Secure South Ridge Video database and then choose Security and Users And Group Accounts from the Tools menu. Delete the Owner user, click Yes, and click OK.

Congratulations! You have completed your Quick Course in Access. By now, you should feel comfortable with all the components of Access, in spite of the complexity of the program and of databases in general. With the basics you have learned here, together with the Help feature and the sample databases that come with the program, you should be able to tackle the creation of some pretty sophisticated databases.

Index

See clearly—
now!

Here's the remarkable, *visual* way to quickly find answers about the powerfully integrated features of the Microsoft® Office 2000 applications. Microsoft Press AT A GLANCE books let you focus on particular tasks and show you, with clear, numbered steps, the easiest way to get them done right now. Put Office 2000 to work today, with AT A GLANCE learning solutions, made by Microsoft.

- MICROSOFT OFFICE 2000 PROFESSIONAL AT A GLANCE
- MICROSOFT WORD 2000 AT A GLANCE
- MICROSOFT EXCEL 2000 AT A GLANCE
- MICROSOFT POWERPOINT® 2000 AT A GLANCE
- MICROSOFT ACCESS 2000 AT A GLANCE
- MICROSOFT FRONTPAGE® 2000 AT A GLANCE
- MICROSOFT PUBLISHER 2000 AT A GLANCE
- MICROSOFT OFFICE 2000 SMALL BUSINESS AT A GLANCE
- MICROSOFT PHOTODRAW® 2000 AT A GLANCE
- MICROSOFT INTERNET EXPLORER 5 AT A GLANCE
- MICROSOFT OUTLOOK® 2000 AT A GLANCE

mspress.microsoft.com

Get a **Free**
e-mail newsletter, updates,
special offers, links to related books,
and more when you
register on line!

Register your Microsoft Press® title on our Web site and you'll get a FREE subscription to our e-mail newsletter, *Microsoft Press Book Connections*. You'll find out about newly released and upcoming books and learning tools, online events, software downloads, special offers and coupons for Microsoft Press customers, and information about major Microsoft® product releases. You can also read useful additional information about all the titles we publish, such as detailed book descriptions, tables of contents and indexes, sample chapters, links to related books and book series, author biographies, and reviews by other customers.

Registration is easy. Just visit this Web page and fill in your information:

http://www.microsoft.com/mspress/register

Microsoft

- -

Proof of Purchase

Use this page as proof of purchase if participating in a promotion or rebate offer on this title. Proof of purchase must be used in conjunction with other proof(s) of payment such as your dated sales receipt—see offer details.

Quick Course® in Microsoft® Access 2000
0-7356-1082-7

CUSTOMER NAME

Microsoft Press, PO Box 97017, Redmond, WA 98073-9830